Becoming an Agent

67

BECOMING AN AGENT

Patterns and Dynamics
for Shaping Your Life

Larry Cochran and Joan Laub

STATE UNIVERSITY OF NEW YORK PRESS

Published by
State University of New York Press, Albany

For information, address State University of New York Press,
State University Plaza, Albany, N.Y., 12246

Production by Cathleen Collins
Marketing by Bernadette LaManna

Library of Congress Cataloging-in-Publication Data

Cochran, Larry, 1944–
    Becoming an agent : patterns and dynamics for shaping your life /
Larry Cochran and Joan Laub.
        p.   cm.
    Includes bibliographical references and index.
    ISBN 0-7914-1719-0 (hard : alk. paper). — ISBN 0-7914-1720-4
(pbk. : alk. paper)
    1. Locus of control—Case studies.   2. Control (Psychology)—Case
studies.   3. Behavior modification—Case studies.   4. Self-
realization—Case studies.   I. Laub, Joan.   II. Title.
BF698.35.L62C63   1993
155.2'5—dc20   93–9163
                                                               CIP

10 9 8 7 6 5 4 3 2 1

Contents

Preface

The enhancement of a person's sense of agency is an important topic in many fields such as rehabilitation, adult education, humanistic psychology, and social work, among others. It is a central focus of counseling psychology and, in particular, of career counseling. Indeed, the general mission of career counseling might be appropriately summarized as helping persons to become agents of their own courses of life, selecting and shaping settings to facilitate more meaningful, productive, and satisfying lives.

This book is concerned with case studies of individuals who made a dramatic change in their lives. In the beginning of the transformation, these persons were living the plot of a patient, victim, or pawn of circumstance. They felt trapped and helpless. In the end, they were living the plot of an agent, actively setting goals, striving, overcoming obstacles, and actualizing ideals. They felt liberated to mold their own courses through life. The aim of this book is to describe what is involved in this remarkable transformation, its organization, pivotal scenes or events, and themes of meaning.

1 / PERSONAL AGENCY

This book is concerned with two major questions. First, what is involved in being an agent or patient of one's career or life? This is a different kind of question than asking what is involved in being an agent when engaged in a clear, definite task such as playing darts, fixing a leaky faucet, or learning to type. Among other things, a definite task involves a specifiable skill, but what skill enables one to be a potent agent in shaping one's course of life? Second, how does a person change from being a patient to being an agent of a life course? To build agency in a practical task, one might instruct and train, cultivate knowledge and skill. To build agency for guiding one's own life, it is not immediately apparent what one should do. Thus, we begin without a clear sense of what agency in life is, or the way in which a person transforms from patiency to agency.

In ordinary language, the concept of agency is reasonably clear. An agent is one who makes things happen and a patient is one to whom things happen. An agent is active while a patient is reactive or passive. A rather lengthy list of distinguishing qualities could be generated easily (decisive, planful, confident, optimistic, etc.), yet such a list would not be expected to apply in every case. Sometimes we emphasize confidence and sometimes we emphasize determination despite a lack of confidence. The concept of agency seems to elude any exact and stable link with a quality such as confidence. Consider, for instance, Rotter's (1966) locus of control of reinforcement. A person with an external locus of control believes

1

that reinforcements are contingent upon luck, chance, fate, and in general, external forces. A person with an internal locus of control believes that reinforcements are contingent upon one's own effort, competence, or influence. Clearly, a person with a greater sense of agency would have an internal locus of control, yet it is obviously unrealistic. As agency is strengthened by a more absolute belief that one controls reinforcements, that there are no external contingencies or forces worth worrying about, one becomes increasingly unrealistic. For this reason, Rotter (1975) suggested that people who have a strong internal locus of control are apt to be maladjusted, as are those with a strong external locus of control. In ordinary language, overconfident and underconfident people are more prone to maladjustment. Suddenly, the middle range becomes desirable. Now, because a sense of agency is virtually defined in isolation by confidence or locus of control, we are put in the odd position of only wanting so much agency, but not too much, of defining agency in a way that is incompatible with realism. The fault seems to lie in attempting to account for agency by a single isolated "mechanism" rather than searching for a synthesis or configuration of features that mutually check and balance one another.

Another problem is that everyone incorporates agency and patiency in daily life. We both do and undergo, yet the ordinary distinction between agents and patients suggests that agency can be enhanced by a simple matter of increasing doing and decreasing undergoing. Such a prescription is impossible. An agent will undergo as much as a patient. The wrong distinction has been made here, and to untangle the concept of agency, one must examine how doing and undergoing are related, or related differently for agents and patients.

As these few illustrations suggest, the concept of agency is problematic, particularly so with regard to a course of life. For example, Bandura (1977) limits self-efficacy (belief that one can successfully complete a task) to specific tasks. Being able to succeed in chess does not necessarily have relevance to self-efficacy in selling used cars. While it has been indicated that one can go beyond a specific task upon the basis of task similarity, such a strategy of generalization only enlarges a sense of agency from a task to a set of tasks. Still left unanswered is the original concern of what it means for a person to be a generally strong or weak agent in living. What are people saying when they report feeling in charge of their lives or like an author of their own destinies? How can one conceive of a more general and enduring sense of agency that could pervade a life rather than being bound to a task or set of tasks?

While this entire book constitutes an attempt to clarify a sense of agency and how it can be enhanced, this chapter provides a selective and critical review of concepts. Our concern is selective in order to shape diverse views into a more coherent starting point for investigation. Our perspective is critical in order to gain distance and flexibility for examining actual cases with more sensitivity. If our initial view were narrow, erring on the side of omission, it would limit further study. If our initial view were too defective, it would misguide investigation. The aim of this chapter, then, is to sketch a perspective on a sense of agency that incorporates other views and that can be examined in actual lives as they are lived.

Action and Agency

The concepts of agency and action are so interrelated that it is difficult to distinguish the enhancement of agency at a time (e.g., in a particular task) from the empowerment or strengthening of action. To enhance agency in, for example, driving a car seems very close indeed to increasing the effectiveness of action in driving. Of course, the concepts differ. A strong sense of agency can endure over lengthy periods of time and in many situations. Customarily, action is restricted to some definite striving to bring about something. While the concepts differ, their borders seem very fluid, perhaps because agency does not involve an agent in isolation or an action in isolation, but rather the character of the agent in relation to the quality of action. In short, agency concerns an agent taking action, but a course of action might be momentary or span years.

Because the borders of the two concepts are so fluid, one can characterize agency by elevating aspects of action into traits of a person. Rather than a persistent action, there is a persistent person. Rather than a goal-directed action, there is a person who shows purpose or commitment. All theories of agency are implicitly or explicitly grounded in the conceptual network of action, a configuration of terms that constitutes an everyday competence in practical understanding (Ricoeur 1984). Even theories that begin with a singular focus, such as self-efficacy, elaborate by gradually encompassing motivation, goals, plans, and other aspects of action (Bandura 1989).

If the major conceptions of agency are generalizations from action, one serving as a model for the other, then one major implication is that personal agency cannot be regarded as a single thing like locus of control, but must be conceived as a complex configuration of parts. No part can be adequately described in isolation from the others for it is the coordination of parts into a functional whole that makes up personal agency. We understand a part through its place within a comprehensible whole.

The aim of this section is to identify and briefly describe the core ingredients of personal agency, as drawn from major theorists. Theorists differ to some extent in the aspects drawn from the conceptual network of action (the overlap is, however, considerable), but largely in the aspects emphasized. Because of this redundancy, we are not concerned here with describing each theory with its distinctive line of research. Rather, we are intent upon the redundancy itself to try for a reasonably broad identification of parts. Indeed, wherever possible, we shall use plain words rather than theoretical terms to entitle a feature. In this way, we can use theories to help compose the central features of agency without prematurely bogging down in theoretical disputes.

Self-determination

For deCharms (1968, 1976), the fundamental condition of agency is an internal locus of causality. The cause of action is within oneself. The person is the origin of action. In contrast, given an external locus of causality, a person feels pushed around like a puppet on a string. Self-determination is not something that can be perceived (after all, a person does not really observe oneself as one observes others), nor deduced with credible potency. Rather, the sense of being the personal cause of one's actions (or more broadly, one's fate) involves a totality of situated experience, more akin to felt judgment, that a person is acting out of his or her own motives. "In short, a person's motives are the reasons for thinking and acting and therefore explain or give meaning to an actor's behavior" (deCharms 1981, p.339)."

As deCharms has refined his theory of personal causation, the meaning of self-determination has expanded through the network of action terms. "The complexity of the origin concept forced us to consider all of the related concepts—choice, freedom, responsibility, and ownership of behavior. The guiding conceptualization was broadened to include them. In a nutshell, originating one's own actions implies choice; choice is experienced as freedom; choice imposes responsibility for choice-related actions and enhances the feeling that the action is 'mine'" (1984, p. 279). In another work, deCharms (1987a) stated that "personal causation means deliberate action to produce intended change" (p. 8). Thus, the experience of being a personal cause is connected with having a meaningful motive, choosing, forming an intention, using knowledge and skill to produce changes (in short, planning), taking responsibility, ownership, and freedom.

Each expansion is problematic. For example, freedom might be conceived as freedom from threats, constraints, and even responsibility. Basically, one seeks escape and might view situations narrowly in terms of barriers or impositions of any form. Such an outlook, however, characterizes a pawn, one with little sense of agency. In contrast, freedom might be conceived as freedom to strive for meaningful goals. One is directed, looking through obstacles for a path toward one's goals. If one is free to pursue one's goal, a person is free enough, so to speak. This sense of freedom is compatible with responsibility for it involves the taking on of responsibility for a course of action. These sorts of distinctions (freedom from versus freedom to) are crucial for resolving the difficulties of expanding personal causation through the network of terms, for sharpening an understanding of agency.

Self-legislation

According to Frankfurt (1971), a distinctive characteristic of human agency is that persons evaluate their own desires, motivations, and choices. Evaluation of one's desires leads to a second order of desire or volition, in which a person wants to have certain kinds of desires or to be free from certain desires. For example, a soldier might yearn for courage, a priest for compassion, or an athlete for discipline. Alternatively, a fashion model might yearn to be rid of a desire for pastry, an academic from the attractions of a more active life, or a judge from sentimentality.

As Taylor (1977) has clarified, a first order evaluation seems more concerned with outcomes. Will one's craving for pastry be more satisfied by a butterhorn or an eclair? Certainly, many views of agency are tied to such a utilitarian outlook. Both self-efficacy (Bandura 1977) and locus of control (Rotter 1966), for instance, are concerned with beliefs that one can complete a task or secure an outcome. The difficulty of such a restriction is that these views neglect meaning, worth, and moral codes, making it impossible to then consider responsibility in any full way. The Marquis de Sade might be just as much a model of agency as Mahatma Gandhi.

Second order evaluations require considerably more depth since what is at issue is not the sheer fact of desire and how it might be satisfied, but the qualitative worth of the desires one has or has not. What qualities should be encouraged and discouraged? Which motives for action are nobler and more base, honorable or dishonorable, virtuous or depraved? Evaluative questions such as these cannot be judged apart from an understanding of the kind of person one wants to be, the kind of life one wants to live. "Our identity is defined by strong evaluations" (Taylor 1977, p. 124). Fundamental evaluations about what ideals and values are to prevail in life are inseparable from a sense of self as agent. Since we decide and act and interpret meanings out of fundamental evaluations, to experience a shattering of or dislodgement from our evaluative constitution as persons would involve a "terrifying breakdown of precisely those capacities which define a human agent" (p. 125).

Amidst the temptations, confusions, conflicts, and distractions of life's options, a person who is to stay on course with some continuity of identity requires a capacity to articulate one's position in deliberation, and to articulate it with the depth necessary to resolve the commensurability of possible courses of action with the desired shape of one's life. When the great German sociologist, Max Weber, was invited to become more active on the national committee for the Democratic party, he tried to explain to a senator why he could not accept this invitation, nor remain on the committee.

> The politician shall and must make compromises. But I am a scholar by profession . . . The scholar dare not make compromises nor cloak any nonsense. I definitely cannot do this. Those who have other views, such as Prof. Lederer and Dr. Vogelstein, are unprofessional. If I acted as they have I would regard myself as a criminal to my profession. (Frye 1967, p. 123)

In this case, the compromises that are necessary and even virtuous in politics are contrasted with the uncompromising character of a scholar. In pursuing the truth, there can be no compromise. One is incommensurable with the other (not reducible to a common measure). If Weber failed to articulate his fundamental evaluations or to do so with the depth necessary to resolve this temptation, he would have endangered his constitution as an agent of his own life. For this reason, among others, Taylor (1977) asserted that "an agent who could not evaluate desires at all would lack the minimum degree of reflectiveness which we associate with a human agent, and would lack a crucial part of the background for what we describe as the exercise of will" (p.117).

Meaningfulness

Both self-determination and self-legislation rest on meaning, and according to Howard (1989), "the most important mechanism humans use to achieve volitional control is meaning" (p.vii). Kobasa (1979) and Maddi (1988) place meaning at the center of commitment and a sense of purpose. Commitment (one of the three components that make up their concept of hardiness) might be summarized as allegiance to one's own distinctive values as they are integrated into a life plan and serve as a basis for involvement in activities. For Werkmeister (1967), "we are not really a person unless we are lawgivers unto ourselves" (p. 127). Restraining, encouraging, and directing desires are intended to help those values to prevail and flourish to which a person stands committed.

For all of these scholars, meaning is concerned with the kind of person one is to be and the kind of life one is to lead. Since meaning transcends the immediate pull of satisfactions to include a past and future, and involves a placement of value upon what is really being achieved in pursuing an immediate desire, meaning concerns a representation of life. But what form does such a representation take?

Werkmeister (1967) has developed a standard or guide for ordering the worth of desires or "felt value experience" from higher to lower. He noted, first, that the literature from diverse cultures, ancient and modern, supports a rough ordering of value experiences, ranging from sense pleasures, gratification of appetites, and a sense of well-being through satisfactions of human interaction, peace of mind, and joys of constructive activities to a sense of self-fulfillment regarding a whole life. What in our experience justifies the ordering that makes the taste of an apple pale alongside the significance of producing a work such as the Table of Elements or *Hamlet*? Werkmeister's answer is that as one goes up the ordering of felt value experiences more of the self is involved and at stake. Lower order value experiences are felt to be tangential to the self. For example, showering after a hot, tiring workout is certainly pleasurable, but one is hardly at stake in any significant way. There is no danger of self-betrayal, but no promise of self-fulfillment. As one moves higher up the ordering, the self becomes more profoundly involved and at stake. Such experiences are more self-defining and life defining. The order of these levels is thus a "measure of the profundity of the self involved in the experience . . . determined by the depth of the involvement of the experiencing self" (p.125).

Intuitively, Werkmeister's ordering is compelling, but it does not provide an individual ordering. To understand why Weber, for instance, felt that the uncompromising stance of a scholar was more meaningful than a compromising stance of a politician, we need a representation that encompasses an agent's actions and experiences over time. Such a representation is a narrative, or as Bruner (1987) stated, "we seem to have no other way of describing lived time save in the form of narrative" (p.12). "Human beings think, perceive, imagine, and make moral judgments according to narrative structures" (Sarbin 1986, p. 8).

The plot of a narrative configures goals, relations, influences, events, circumstances, and actions, among other things, into a temporal whole (Polkinghorne 1988). In particular, characters are aligned in story and a person assumes one of the prominent roles. According to MacIntyre (1984), "the self inhabits a character whose unity is given as the unity of character" (p. 217). Summed up most directly by Howard (1989), "a life becomes meaningful when one sees himself or herself as an actor within the context of a story" (p. vii).

Thus, Weber rejected the compromising acts of a politician because they clashed with the narrative plot of a German scholar uncompromisingly (that is, with integrity) searching for truth. In a political plot, a compromise might be regarded as an act of brilliant leadership or statesmanship, but in a scholarly plot it reflects a loathsome lack of integrity. In this way, the configuration of character in a story provides the basis for shaping oneself to play a part and shaping the life one leads.

Purposefulness

People set goals and strive to reach them. In this sense, everyone is purposive. However, people vary in the nature of the goals established. Some are filled with a sense of purpose; others are alienated from their own goals and lack a sense of purpose or commitment (Kobasa 1979). What are the differences between goals that enhance the sense of being a purposeful human agent and goals that undermine this sense?

In the context of a human life, a goal is a symbolic vehicle for transforming ideals into actualities. Human existence involves a chronic double vision of ideal and actual. We have an actual self-concept and an ideal self-concept. We assess life as it is actually lived alongside our vision of a good life. Double vision allows us to see into situations with a depth that would be denied a being with no capacity for idealization. Through contrast, we construe our own incompletion, erecting gaps between what is and what ought to be (Cochran 1985). Gaps are experienced as disturbances, yearnings, upsets, disenchantments, and conflicts, all moving a person toward completion, the actualization of what is better or more ideal. In personality theory, this portrait is the general basis for what Maddi (1980) terms the perfection theorists such as Adler (1956), Allport (1955, 1961), and Maddi (1970) himself. The fundamental striving of a human being is toward completion through actualizing the ideal. In this sense, goals are representations of possible completion (Maddi 1988).

According to this perspective, there are two fundamental aspects of setting agentic goals. First, is the goal anchored in a strong theme of meaning? Does it constitute a translation, really, of meaning into a goal (deCharms 1976)? The goal might be individually constructed, set by context (work, tradition, etc.) or even imposed by others, and these differences might indeed alter one's sense of agency in taking action, but the main consideration is whether a goal emerges from meaningful motives. Second, the goal is possible. Drawing from work on the achievement motive (McClelland 1961), deCharms (1976) argues persuasively that challenging goals are more agentic, goals that are difficult but achievable. This point has been supported extensively through research on goal setting (Lee, Locke, and Latham 1989; Locke and Latham 1984). Goals that are too extravagant or too trivial simply lack a serious appraisal of reality and make commitment rather doubtful. The extravagant goal, for instance, is too close to an unrealistic wish, insufficiently anchored as a definite possibility for which to strive. Then too, its very improbability moves too easily into excuse making, impressing others with goals rather than attainments, and justification for giving up. The trivial goal is too easily attained, not requiring a strong exercise of agency and probably not capable of actualizing ideals very powerfully. Certainly, there are other features of goals to consider such as goal specificity or the integration of short-term and long-term goals, but the meaningfulness and challenge of a goal seem to be the most critical features for agency.

In Maddi (1988) and Kobasa's (1979) concept of hardiness, an important component is a disposition to view change as a challenge "At the core of the search for novelty and challenge are fundamental life goals that have become increasingly integrated in a widening diversity of situations" (Kobasa 1979, p.4). Perhaps seeking challenge should be made into a separate feature of agency, but it is so interrelated with purposefulness that it is difficult to separate. In a situation, a person might seek meaningful opportunities and challenges, but these are apt to amount to the same thing, and in any case, come together as a goal.

Confidence

Agency theorists such as Bandura (1989) and Rotter (1966) have tended to be concerned with what Frankfurt (1971) termed first order desires, essentially a utilitarian outlook. In this case, confidence is concerned with a person's capacity in relation to desired outcomes such as success or attaining positive consequences. Does a person have the capacity to make a difference in the course of events, to influence what happens that affects his or her life? Confidence is concerned with a person's trust in and reliance upon oneself to get things done, to act effectively. The opposite of confidence might be learned helplessness (Seligman 1975).

While Bandura and Rotter focus upon a belief that one can control outcomes, emphasizing the Platonic separation of cognition, emotion, and conation, deCharms (1981, 1984, 1987a, 1987b) stresses the experienced totality of confidence and other features of agency. For deCharms, confidence is not just a matter of belief, nor is it just an inference from observation. Rather, it concerns the whole quality of experience as lived, more akin to a felt judgment or part of an orientation. Conceiving and feeling are united in taking a position or making a valuative judgment (Cochran 1985), and this emphasis upon the quality of experience is more congruent with such intimate terms as trust, reliance, or faith. The difficulty with the emphasis upon belief is that the term is so ambiguous. Beliefs might be superficial or deep, implicit or explicit, impassioned or dry, fragile in the face of reality or unshakable, and professed more than acted upon. Better distinctions are needed to use the term with much assurance.

A second difficulty is that this view of confidence neglects second order desires, those concerned with evaluating the desires one has or lacks. From a second order perspective, confidence would concern faith, trust, or assurance in the desires one has or the course of action one is following, more like confidence in a right direction. Confidence of this kind might be maintained regardless of success or failure, positive or negative consequences. Among notable figures, Mahatma Gandhi illustrates this order of confidence. Here, there is no necessary assurance that one can make a difference, but there is assurance that one will try, and assurance in a higher vision that deserves or is meant to prevail.

Active striving

Given the disparity between the actual and ideal, what is and what ought to be, a person with a stronger sense of agency takes a more active posture, perhaps as one more accustomed to actualizing the ideal. DeCharms (1976) found that striving emerged as the major difference between agents and patients. Agents take action while patients endure or seem more passive in response to disparity between the actual and ideal.

Further, agents tend to be more proactive than reactive (deCharms 1987a). The difference is that reactions are guided by external circumstances while proactions are guided by individual purpose in light of circumstances. Thus, someone who simply reacts is apt to lose sight of meaningful possibilities, acting on urgencies, obstacles, and opportunities as they arise. Unguided by a sense of purposefulness, a person reacts to or against circumstance. Guided by a sense of purposefulness, a person is apt to view circumstances in a more balanced perspective. Obstacles are restraints to move through or around to attain goals. Opportunities are sized up in relation to priorities and purposes. Having a purpose encourages a balanced response to circumstances, allowing a person to stay on course. Lacking a purpose encourages imbalanced reactions for there is no clear course to be on or off.

From a utilitarian perspective, striving is grounded in confidence. Given a belief that one has the capacity to succeed in various tasks, a person is encouraged to strive and persevere. From the second order or, what might be termed, a moral perspective, striving is apt to be grounded more in meaningfulness and purposefulness. One strives because it is the right thing to do. There are ideals worth striving to actualize, not necessarily because their attainment is probable, but because their actualization is right or good and giving up amounts to yielding to wrong or bad. In both cases, however, the mark of an agent is that he or she takes active steps toward goals.

Planfulness

Planning involves realistic appraisal and the construction of a course of action. Planning links what a person wants to the realities of a context, in the form of a planned course of action. Like goal setting, planning mediates between the actual and ideal. Planning is part of agency for the rather obvious reason that agents take action, and they cannot take very effective courses of action without planning.

DeCharms (1976) refers to planning as reality perception, the appraisal of means, obstacles, constraints, opportunities, interpersonal influences, and resources. Contexts are sized up realistically according to what will facilitate and hinder movement toward a goal. While deCharms emphasized realism, we prefer the concept of planning for it indicates what realistic appraisal is for.

Phrased most directly and simply, if a person is serious about actualizing an ideal or achieving a goal, he or she will assess realities to devise ways the goal might be achieved. If one's motivation is not serious, there is no need to take reality into account in this way. There are an endless number of ways in which the realities of context might be experienced. One person might be alert for restrictions of any kind, feeling unfair infringements at every opportunity. Another person might be alert for offenses or attention or fun, and so on. Of course, strong agents are not immune to highlighting features of reality in diverse ways, but when pursuing a meaningful goal, reality is ordered in a particular way. Namely, planning is a kind of plot construction that configures ingredients of reality along a story line. For example, if one wanted to get good grades, the basic story line is set. Realities become relevant to this line of intent to the extent that they facilitate or hinder movement. A chatty acquaintance, the quality of one's study lamp, sleeping habits, recreational interests such as listening to music, noise, and the like might all configure in the plot to get good grades. Planning is a way to configure an agentic plot in which some things are minimized or eliminated while other things are enhanced to attain a goal.

Spivack, Platt, and Shure (1976) have argued, and provided reasonable evidence, that adjustment depends upon problem-solving capability, involving certain skills such as means-end thinking, generation of solutions, and causal thinking. However, in learning these skills, a person comes to resemble very closely what is meant by an agent, particularly in the way planning is developed from impoverished narratives to richer, more flexible narratives. Thus, it could be reasonably argued that agentic motivation enhances skills, which in turn strengthen an agentic posture. If one were acting as an agent, planning and striving to achieve meaningful goals, skills of planning or problem solving would be precisely those that would be exercised and developed.

Responsibility

Several senses of responsibility are relevant to agency. First, if a person experienced self-determination in setting a course of action, he or she would be responsible for it, and liable to respond to deviations off course or necessities for readjusting one's course of action. Second, if one believes that a successful outcome or positive consequences are within one's control, one is then responsible for a successful outcome or consequences, barring unforeseen circumstances and developments. Without the power to make a difference, one cannot be responsible.

These senses of responsibility seem reasonably clear although they can become muddled in experience. For example, do we take responsibility for unintended consequences? It all depends, but on what? Sometimes, unintended consequences are contingent affairs that could hardly be foreseen. Sometimes, they are more necessarily tied to intended consequences and should have been foreseen. As another example, it can be much more agentic to claim exact responsibility rather than just more responsibility. Suppose a student received a poor grade on a test. By accepting or denying responsibility, in a general way, a person is in no better position to study effectively for the next test. However, by examining the situation in a more balanced and realistic way, one might be able to see that one's failure was due to a neglect of basic terms, inadequate review, incomplete understanding, low investment of time, and so on. In this sense, assigning exact responsibility for poor performance is empowering since it can lead to corrective efforts, to understand exactly where one can take responsibility for doing better. Alternatively, one might discover that the teacher made the test tricky and no one did well. In this case, one is empowered not to do better, but through being alleviated of responsibility for a result that did not reflect one's capabilities and efforts. Both of these instances call for judgment and for a just discernment of reality, of what is really the case, and both are clearly connected with agency. For these kinds of reasons, no glib pronouncement about the role of responsibility is possible. It is more the case that an agent searches for what one can be responsible for. What one can take responsibility for, one can change, whether it be concerned with first order or second order desires. Taking responsibility, then, emerges as an exacting task of one disposed to making things happen. To err on the side of lack of responsibility blinds one from exercises of agency that could make a difference. To err on the side of taking too much responsibility leads one toward futile exercises of agency.

Commentary

Perhaps the most striking quality of these agentic features is their interdependence, which is unsurprising if most or all make up the conceptual network of action. For example, action requires a goal and if that goal is set too high or too low, action is doomed to futility or triviality. A particular feature cannot be adequately framed apart from other features. Indeed, it became clear that there is considerable potential for incompatibility without the right stresses and exact distinctions. For example, not all senses of freedom fit harmoniously with responsibility. Overconfidence clashes with the realism necessary for serious planning. Goals can be alienating if not anchored in meaning. And so on.

This interdependence of agentic features also indicates that no feature adequately accounts for agency. For example, one might have efficacious beliefs and still feel powerless. As a young man, Saint Augustine (1961) was successful in his work as a teacher and in lustful pursuits, but felt trapped and helpless. He felt a slave to ambitions and passions that were worthless and meaningless, and he scorned his capacity to satisfy these ambitions and passions. "Eager for fame and wealth and marriage" (p. 118), and clearly capable of actualizing these ambitions, Saint Augustine could but feel that his "misery was complete" (p. 118). Similarly, one might have an enhanced sense of meaning, seeing oneself as the main character in a fine drama, but meaningfulness takes on the status of a daydream unless it is acted upon, is filled out with goals, plans, choices, and actions. Alone, each feature has obvious counterexamples to undermine any presumption that agency is just a matter of confidence, responsibility, or whatever. If this is so, a sense of agency is concerned with an integration of agentic features, a whole rather than a collection of parts.

While agentic features are interdependent and this interdependence seems necessary to understand a sense of agency, the examination has only yielded parts with only a vague sense of what the whole might be. The analysis into parts has not as yet led to a way to form a synthesis. However, three valuable criteria have emerged to guide such a synthetic effort.

First, a sense of agency is concerned with meaning, or a unifying theme of meaning composed of several strands. A sense of agency is not, for instance, the property of an organism. To properly assess a person's sense of agency, we need to understand that person's orientation. Responsibility, goals, intention, and the like, all concern meaning from the perspective of the agent. Second, an agent is thoroughly contextualized. Outside of a situation or context of some kind, there is no conceivable agent. Or arrived at in another way, agency is always exercised in relation to context, and context offers its own contributions to meaning.

Third, a sense of agency is lived or experienced; it is not just a dry belief. This criterion greatly restricts compositions of meaning that are applicable to a sense of agency. There are compositions that ordinarily cannot be lived such as the chemical composition of a plant, a map of a territory, or a mathematical series. Such knowledge might figure in agency as means, but is not livable (except perhaps through intuitive and imaginative processes). However, a narrative composition can be lived. The dramatic plots of Horatio Alger novels, for instance, were lived by large numbers of people. Further, narrative emplots characters in context and forms a unifying theme of meaning, capable of unifying quite diverse strands. Narrative is probably the only composition that is capable of satisfying the three criteria presented here, with the possible exception of metaphor.

Story and Agency

To describe an action or course of action is to tell a story. To describe the successful action of a potent agent is to tell a story with a strong agentic plot. Ordinarily, to represent agency, we portray the kind of plot in which an agent figures as a main character. Certainly, one might attempt to represent agency in other ways such as mathematical formulas or flow diagrams, but these are special representations for a very restricted audience. The ordinary, everyday form of representation is narrative (Polkinghorne 1988).

A narrative representation not only offers a way of understanding, a meaningful interpretation of experience, but guides action. To enact a story, one follows the plot in one's interpretations and actions. Narrative constitutes a synchronic structure that is diachronically unfolded as an intelligible replication of itself in perhaps novel circumstances. From a realist's perspective on science (Manicas and Secord 1983), a narrative plot is a powerful particular (Harre 1974), a real causal structure that shapes the course of action over time. Shaping is evident in both the course pursued and corrections taken when one deviates or moves off course. From this perspective, agency is grounded in the plots a person follows in daily life.

Agentic Plots

A story is organized around the opposition of beginning and end. The beginning has been traditionally characterized as an upset, disequilibrium, disturbance, or conflict, a gap between what is and what ought to be. The end brings closure to what was aroused in the beginning. There is some latitude in what might count as an ending, particularly since the nature of the beginning might be elaborated throughout the story. For example, if one lost a job, a person might find a job, become resolved to unemployment, or gain a recreational activity. There are many possible endings for any beginning, but each would constitute a form of opposition.

The middle of a story concerns how a person moved from a particular beginning to a particular end. Since beginning and end offer two poles of an opposition, a coherent and potentially rigorous guide is offered to determine the relevance of events, people, and circumstances. If an element did not bear upon the movement toward or away from the end, it would lack relevance and could be edited out of the story. The middle is more than a chronology; it involves a plot that explains how the end came about (Danto 1985), showing the causal significance of parts as they configure in a whole account of the change.

An agentic plot can be filled in by both theory and research. Theoretically, for instance, a Bandura tale would almost certainly emphasize perseverence despite setbacks. A Taylor plot would involve allegiance to ideals that define a person and a course of life. For a little more detail, consider Maddi (1988) as a script writer for agentic plots. Within this theory, patients are stuck in "facticity" (the fixed and unchangeable) while agents explore and actualize possibilities. Through cultivating symbolization (more refined representation), imagination (to conceive of possibility), and judgment (to distinguish what is fixed and what is possible), the central task of an agent is to discern meaningful possibilities to guide courses of action. In such a plot, there are discoveries of two types. One might discover that what seemed fixed is really changeable or discover that what seemed possible is really limited or fixed. Whether encouraging or discouraging, agents continue exploring to shape the most meaningful life that is possible. Pivotal kinds of events would include timely support from others, mastery experiences that enhance a sense of competency and increased possibility, and experiences of change that are enriching rather than chaotic. Rather than experiencing change and novelty as threats, a hardy agent would search for opportunities, feel challenged to vigorously search for and act on new possibilities. There would be more experiences that seem worthwhile and interesting, and a more active, involved orientation to making things happen. In short, the plot would depend in part upon the planning, organizing, and doing of the agent, all with a more uplifting anticipation that it is within one's power to make a happy ending more likely.

While theorists have not specified details of an agentic plot, each is quite suggestive regarding what such a plot would be.

Empirically, there are numerous studies that might help fill in an agentic plot. One of the most comprehensive efforts is the strangely neglected work of Arnold (1962) on constructive motivation. Using Murray's (1943) Thematic Apperception Test, she elicited stories from individuals. Viewing each story as the exploration of a problem and its resolution, she formulated the import or moral of the story to reveal a conviction of the storyteller, a motivational pattern or principle of action. Given several stories from a person, the sequence of imports reveals a fuller range of convictions about moral conduct, reaction to adversity, what leads to success and failure, and other people. For example, below are the first two stories from a fifteen-year-old female. She had recently moved to a new school where she was repeating grade nine. According to her school counselor, she was doing poorly and might have to repeat grade nine again if her motivation did not improve.

"This young child has just received an assignment from his music teacher to play in front of the class. He goes home and tries writing something that he can play and accomplish, and also please the teacher. The night before the big day he grows excited at the thought of getting a chance to prove himself to the teacher. That night, his mom wants him to practice and be prepared, but he decides to go outside and play with friends. His mom gets mad, but tells him to decide for himself. When he comes in, his mom wants him to practice, but he is tired, so goes to bed. In the morning, he rushes around, trying to get prepared to present the composition and his mother tells him just to do his best and don't rush it."

"After teaching a class, the teacher was totally exhausted. Outside, the teacher started walking with a mother toward the edge of town where the mother lived. On the way, they had an argument over the way the teacher was teaching the children. The teacher argued with the mother over the way she raised her children. The mother was stubborn and became angry while the teacher was frustrated and confused at the thought that the mother had a higher priority for farming than for school."

The imports for these stories seem reasonably clear. "While you might get excited about proving yourself by performing well, you play instead despite the urgings of others, and have to rush to prepare at the last minute." Here, there is an initial desire that does not come to fruition. Instead of taking adequate means to perform well, the main character becomes distracted in play and too tired to practice. What is the consequence for neglecting adequate practice or abandoning a desire? It might be failure, an embarrassing performance, letting oneself down, and so on. But in the story, the only consequence is that he has to rush to prepare. Dismal preparation leads only to a last minute rush.

The second story explores achievement further. What if one did work hard? "Even if you work yourself to exhaustion, people will criticize and downgrade your work, and you will end up frustrated and confused." Phrased in the idiom of the age group, if you slack off in work, nothing much really happens. However, if you knock yourself out working, you will be put down anyway. As convictions, principles of action or inaction, it is of little wonder why she was doing poorly in school.

Just as the import or moral is derived from story, a proverblike statement of a story's point, an import might be filled out in story, providing a skeletal plot for development. From Arnold's work, it is as if a person held a repertoire of plots, only some of which would serve as a basis for action. For example, the girl above would not be likely to work hard if, in her view, working led to criticism and downgrading. In contrast, she would be more likely to play or engage in immediate attractions because there is no strongly negative outcome for lack of effort. Throughout all of her stories, there was no positive outcome, only negative and neutral ones. Perhaps she has no credible plot for a positive outcome. Since there is nothing to compel her effort, it is as if immediate attractions win by default.

Based on her research, Arnold (1962) compiled a system of categories for scoring the imports of stories. Imports that reflect constructive motivation are scored 2 or 1. Imports that reflect destructive motivation are scored -2 or -1. There are four main divisions (achievement, right versus wrong, human relationships, and reaction to adversity), each with a number of subdivisions. To score a story, one looks up the subdivision that is most similar to the import and uses the examples to guide scoring. For example, under the subdivision of means taken toward a goal, an import is scored 2 if success came through active effort or adequate means, or if failure came through inadequate effort, impulsive action, negative attitudes, or improbable and deficient means. An import is scored -2 if success came through fantasy (magic, heavenly reward, etc.) or despite antisocial (e.g., dishonest) or ineffective means (despite disinterest, playing, sleeping, etc.), or if failure came through adequate effort and effective means. A person's overall score is the sum of import scores, usually for ten stories. In several astonishingly powerful studies of validity, Arnold has been able to distinguish people who show excellence in teaching, academic achievement (from elementary school through college), adjustment, and effectiveness in executive performance. The plots that people use in telling imaginative stories appear to be enacted in daily life.

Character and Plot

Within a culture, there is a large repertoire of stories that guide the participation of members and allow other members to interpret that participation in an intelligible way (Turner and Bruner 1986). Within this culture, for instance, the Horatio Alger stories inspired youth to live agentic plots. For example, in Norman Vincent Peale's (1984) autobiography, he recalled the influence of Alger's novels. "I happen to have grown up and to have formed my life philosophy in a period when the Horatio Alger 'strive and succeed' work ethic was universally believed in; when individual study and effort were honored; when to make something of your potential was highly regarded" (p. 26). However, people do not live all the culturally patterned plots to which they are exposed. Partially, plot enactment is restricted by available settings (i.e., we have to be in the right setting for a story line), social class (Willis 1977), family (MacGregor and Cochran 1988), and historical period (Turner 1974). Of particular importance in restricting plots a person might enact is one's reflexive appraisal of his or her own character.

Plotting includes the prospect of taking a particular role in story. A plot requires or calls for a particular kind of role for the main character, just as a particular role calls for a certain kind of plot. Character and plot must cohere to be intelligible. The story form of an agent, for instance, involves firm intention cast against the resistance of other people, unfavorable circumstances, and weaknesses of one's own character. To actualize his or her purpose, an agent must take action, strive, resist temptation, absorb disappointment, and struggle to overcome barrier after barrier to stay on course. In contrast, according to Weston's (1970) study of literature, the story form of a patient involves vague hope cast within engaging circumstances. There is not so much a definite intention as a general hope to escape or avoid the worst. Through one threat after another, a patient reacts and undergoes until a final salvation or resignation is reached. The tale of a patient portrays intense and varied reactions. A much more sophisticated study of character and plot can be found in Frye's (1957) renowned work, but the principle is the same. Character and plot must fit in an intelligible way, and each is incomplete without the other.

Whether a person feels suited for a part depends upon whether he or she can fulfill what the role requires. Alternatively, typecasting oneself restricts the plots that can be realistically envisioned. "People's perceptions of their efficacy influences the types of anticipatory scenarios they construct and reiterate" (Bandura 1989, p. 1176). For example, if a person did not believe that he or she could coach a baseball team very well, the person might generate deviant plots filled with mishaps, embarrassments, and failures. Suitability for a part also depends upon whether the role is congruent with personal ideals, among other things. However, it serves no immediate purpose to elaborate aspects of suitability further at this point.

The formation of plots to enact seems to require a holistic appreciation of self and situation that takes into account many different ingredients such as means, purpose, and audience (consult Burke 1969). Plotting is a fallible activity. The synthesis formed might be filled with errors of omission and commission. One might ignore or neglect confidence if allegiance to ideals is at stake, or vice versa. Plotting involves the construction of meaning. Since the configurative activity of emplotment is concerned with adjustments of meaning within an emerging whole, it is difficult to conceive of features of a person as isolated variables that have causal impact upon one another. The current language of efficient causality seems ill-suited for a configuration of meaning, particularly with its tendency to reify abstractions. Let us treat statements such as "self-esteem affects future outlook" or "self-efficacy affects the level of goal-setting" as only a manner of speaking, a shorthand really that must be unpacked in a configuration of meaning to make any sense.

Of much more appropriateness is the language of wholes stemming from Gestalt psychology (e.g., Ellis 1967). Underlying the various laws formulated in Gestalt psychology is the Law of Good Gestalt or Law of Pregnance (consult Fuller's seminal work 1990). Within any creation or actualization of meaning, there is a lawful tendency for that configuration of meaning to move toward the best meaning possible, in which parts come increasingly to fit together, to cohere rather than be out of place. Given that a plot is a form of gestalt, there is a tendency for the parts of a plot of configure in the direction of the best fit possible. Thus, if we have a confident person setting trivial goals, the parts do not fit together. Adjustments of meaning in the right direction are called for to move toward a better plot. Of course, the defective whole is the traditional beginning of story, calling for a movement toward a better whole (a point that will be discussed in some detail later).

Following a Plot

Given the situation in which a person has a more or less definite plot, following it is partially a matter of enacting what is required of one's role according to a particular view of what produces what. A plot is not just one thing after another, but one thing because of another (e.g., Ricoeur 1984). A plot is like a theory of what leads from a particular beginning to a particular end. Every action or event within the plot is directed, meaning that to follow a plot allows one to be coherently oriented, able to specify or sense the relation of a particular action to the movement of the whole.

In some ways, following a plot is like following a plan. However, an agent tends to be conscious of a plan while it is not the case that an agent necessarily must be conscious of the full plot. This point requires illustration. In a study of career change, Chusid and Cochran (1989) found that in working, people enacted dramas learned within one's family of origin, or more broadly, dramas learned in growing up. In the first case study of Alice, her mother dominated the family by acting like a victim. The mother acted resentfully, maliciously, and negatively, as one who had been victimized by the world. Alice's role was to motivate her mother to be more positive, and in particular, to appease her by "always putting out," never demanding or threatening. As Alice struggled to keep mother together and to appease her, she felt weak and oppressed, pushed to have some life of her own. "It is a feeling of pulling things out of myself. The word that comes to mind is it's not good enough. Keep trying harder and harder, forever putting out . . . really busting your gut." The dominant theme of this drama was constant struggle to appease a tyrant who ruled through playing victim.

> For Alice, the world of architects involved those who were "getting used and those who were handing it out," people like her mother who were "nonsupports, takers, and no heart." Being an architect required a pulling out of yourself to put it on paper . . . It was very, very frustrating. It was on your shoulders, and it was like an albatross. At the same time, it wouldn't let go. I remember just working 36 hours straight. I redesigned X eight times; each time for different reasons, something had to change. As with her mother, "no matter how hard you tried, it was never good enough." In both, she felt under the power of demanding people, forced to perform and no matter how much she produced, more was demanded. (Chusid and Cochran 1989, p. 37)

As with other participants in the study, Alice was not explicitly aware of the plot she was living out in work. She was aware of aspects, but not the whole and not the origin of the plot in her family of origin. Even when she used virtually the same terms to describe her mother and coworkers, her struggle to appease, she did not make the connection. Yet in her narrative accounts of work and home life, and in her Q-sorts of mother and coworkers, the similarity in pattern was striking. Some aspects of the original plot were altered or eliminated, but substantially the same plot was enacted in work. When the parallel was brought to her attention, her reaction was intense, as were those of other participants. They cried, laughed enthusiastically, were overjoyed and saddened. They seemed to experience insight and recognition at the same time.

From this and other studies (e.g., Csikszentmihalyi and Beattie 1979; Ochberg 1987; Osherson, 1980), people seem to enact plots, but do not necessarily have a full and explicit grasp of those plots.

There are several other indicators of how a plot differs from a plan. First, people often switched roles in a drama. For example, in growing up, Kay was controlled and invalidated by her mother at seemingly every turn. She had to perform responsibly, but without autonomy. With her grandmother, however, she was accepted in a playful, loving atmosphere and could be herself. As a preschool supervisor, Kay enacted the role of her grandmother to children who were like herself as a daughter, but under the supervision of a boss who resembled mother. While a similar story is evident, Kay now has a different role in the story, altering her participation in the enactment of a plot. While one can switch roles in a coordinated plan, the aim is the same. However, switching roles in a plot can change a person's aims, ideals, and required characteristics.

A second difference between a plot and a plan is that a plot configures more into the whole. A plan is largely a functional arrangement of tasks to accomplish something. Indeed, planning and following a plan might be configured in a plot. However, a plot includes emotions, styles of role enactment, and in general, meaning as lived. A deliberate plan cannot credibly account for many pivotal aspects of a plot which are concerned with passions. For example, Alice (in the example above) cannot credibly plan for a feeling of pulling more out of herself. Now is the time to feel this or that, would she say? It is much too stagy and inauthentic, but time after time, a person does go through essentially the same story with often a vivid sense of authenticity.

A third difference is that it is normal to remind oneself of one's plan. One can become lost or lose one's place and refer to the plan to know what to do next. However, in following a plot, one has no reminder. It follows naturally more like a well-practiced skill. Using Polanyi's (1967) distinction, a plan can be examined as an explicit focus of attention that one deliberately follows. A plot forms a tacit ground for interpreting, feeling, and acting. We attend from a tacit plot to concrete details of situations, shaping them into the narrative pattern.

A final difference is that a plan is intended to help achieve something. In contrast, a plot might or might not be positive. For example, Alice felt oppressed. She did not want to go through life struggling to appease heartless exploiters. Kay felt frustrated. While she wanted to help others (who resembled herself as a daughter), she did not want to be under the authority of a motherlike figure. Through becoming a stockbroker, Alice was able to replot her career with a drama that emphasized autonomy, distance from others, and neutrality in relationships. Kay also switched jobs, but ended up in the same frustrating plot. Only the setting and people changed. Both were painfully aware of the importance of changing, but not fully or coherently aware of the plot they were living. They had little sense of their own contributions to this experience. Neither Alice nor Kay consciously tried to recreate in work a drama of youth. If they had known, they would have rejected it and tried to live in a different way.

Following a plot emerges as a more complicated activity than might have been imagined. While one might try to follow a plot as if it were a plan or set of instructions, this level could only be regarded as preliminary or perhaps transitional. It is too superficial. More deeply, one might follow a plot as one would an imaginative activity of pretense or playacting. Certainly, children are able to engage in taking imaginative roles quite early. The concept of imitation, with its image of a fixed behavior being duplicated, scarcely covers the ingenuity and novelty that are involved in pretense. However, we usually know when we are pretending, and even in adult cases where people enact public personas, it can be set aside. At the deepest level of following a plot, one cannot easily set it aside and, indeed, might struggle against it or against what one knows of it (also consult Sloan 1986). A plot seems to emerge as part of a tacit ground of orientation that specifies what the world is like, what other people are like, and what oneself is like.

Authoring a Plot

Following a plot is partially a matter of authoring as one goes along, for at least two reasons. First, plots might be more or less complete. Gaps are apt to be common, requiring a person to fill in the plot in a consistent way, as the need arises. Second, acting in varying contexts offers novelties and differences that could scarcely be foreseen. There are also apt to be setbacks, discrepancies, and recalcitrant features of reality that require plot extension or refinement. Even if a plot seems reasonably comprehensive, the novelties of context virtually assure that it would be incomplete. In short, things simply cannot be expected to go exactly as anticipated, at least for much of the time. Because of unexpected complications, some degree of authoring is required to follow a plot.

Authoring a story line is conducted through interpreting and acting (consult Carr 1986). That is, one works directly upon a narrative representation to incorporate features of reality or one acts to shape reality in accordance with a representation. As an illustration, consider role alignment, following McCall and Simmons' (1966) analysis of role-identity negotiations. Suppose Jane enacts the role of boss. One cannot do this very well in isolation. She needs other people who will fill the role of follower or subordinate. Thus, through her manner and actions, she presents herself as a boss, inviting others to take the role of follower, to which they have been cast by her plot. However, others have their own script and are busy trying to cast her in a particular role as well. In short, they might resist depiction as a supportive follower, a reluctant follower who has to be watched, a rebellious subordinate, an underminer, or any of the familiar variants of the follower role that are familiar to Jane. They can always be edited out of the plot enactment as irrelevant oddities, but also Jane might try to make sense of them in a different way. For instance, she might improvise a new type of follower such as an independent subordinate who needs some "slack" and must be handled with care. Alternatively, she might coerce, intimidate, persuade, bribe, or charm people into showing more deference to her. To author others in relevant roles, a person acts as a participant in a story and stands back as a spectator on the story for broader interpretation.

Stemming from Britton (1970), Harding (1937), and Arendt (1978), a spectator is temporarily withdrawn from the affairs of the world, not seeking to get anything done. Unpressured by urgent requirements of the moment to get something done, a spectator is able to take a broader perspective on events, drawing upon ideals and understandings of a more total worldview. A spectator interprets, appreciates, elaborates, and integrates in recounting or representing experience. Spectatorship is a way to restore one's representation. Through operating upon one's representation (e.g., plot or story), a person attempts to incorporate shocks and novelties within a whole, to explore possibilities, and to evaluate the significance of ideals in events. Restoring a representation is a restoration of a livable plot. Some restorations might be far-reaching, calling for more than corrections of a plot, but of change to another plot (Spence 1982). A participant is immersed in the affairs of the world, trying to get things done. Narrowed in perspective by the urgent demands of action, a participant does not operate on a representation, but rather uses a representation to guide action. A participant plans, decides, and acts. Participation is a way to enact and actualize a representation. Through operating on and in the world, a participant masters roles and competencies, tests possibilities, and shapes reality and a way of living.

As Britton (1970) has emphasized, drawing from Kelly (1955) and Piaget (1968), the roles of a participant and spectator are not really two separate modes of authorship, but more like poles of a continual cycle. Our participation in events generates material for standing back to make sense of things while our onlooking generates material to enact. Feeble enactment is apt to impoverish onlooking (at least as regards actualizing goods) just as feeble onlooking might impoverish enactment. A sense of agency cannot be contrasted with a spectator role for agency (in the sense of authorship), depends upon spectatorship. The role of a patient is not the same as the role of a spectator, nor can a sense of agency be bound to the role of a participant. Rather, a sense of agency is concerned not just with the content of plots narrated and enacted, but with the resilience and vigor of the cycle of participant and spectator that enhances authorship.

Summary

Let us summarize the argument thus far. In examining attributes of agency, we have found that each attribute is incomplete, requiring others to balance it and sharpen its role within a configuration. Within an agentic configuration, some features or attributes might even be absent in some cases. The kind of synthesis that is most appropriate for considering a sense of agency is a story form. One can hold and enact agentic plots, and there are many culturally patterned narratives to serve as models. However, no plot that a person follows, either explicitly or implicitly, is complete. To follow a plot requires ongoing authorship to stay on course, and authorship depends upon spectatorship as well as participation. Despite the indefinite number of complications that might throw one off course or that must be configured in plot, the activity of plotting and ongoing authorship seems to conform to the Gestalt Law of Pregnance, of meaningful actualizations moving toward the best configuration possible. And this movement can be discerned by examining the alteration of parts (self-determination, confidence, etc.) as they mutually adjust to one another in the whole. In short, we have moved from attributes to plots to plotting.

That story is the critical form through which a sense of agency can be understood provides a coherent focus for studying a transformation of agency. In changing from a patient to an agent, we are not concerned so much with increasing the number of tasks in which a person feels confident. After all, there is no practical end to tasks. Rather, we are concerned with the kind of role a person adopts in a story line that he or she lives, and story can encompass a course of life (Cochran 1990). It is not a matter of generalizing from success on a few tasks to tasks in general, but of being able to fulfill a role in story that moves toward a particular end. A role requires certain tasks to be performed, among other things, but these tasks would be definite and bounded. However, with a narrative focus, an understanding of transformation must go beyond tasks to other questions concerned with a redramatization of life.

2 / ENHANCING AGENCY

How does a person change from a patient to an agent in shaping and living a course of life? The aim of this chapter is to explore this question in preparation for examining actual cases of persons who have made such a transformation. From the perspective of the previous chapter, to change from a patient to an agent is to adopt or elaborate an agentic plot that the person lives (Howard 1989). If a person lacks such a plot, he or she must construct one. If a person has an agentic plot that is not quite workable, he or she must extend or refine the plot in ways that allow agency to be more fully exercised. If a person is hindered due to allegiance to a faulty plot, one must revise it. Minimally, the change from patient to agent requires the composition of a story line, motivation for a particular role, and mastery of that role.

Agentic Experiences

From research literature, there are at least three kinds of experiences that foster agency. In each case, the general principle is that a person becomes more agentic through enacting an agentic orientation. Becoming an agent is a straightforward matter of effective or successful practice. At least, let us begin with this simple principle and complicate the account as we are required to do so by problems.

Each form of experience involves a progression from models of agency, imaginative rehearsal of agency, preparatory practice of relevant knowledge and skill, and actual enactments, leading to reflection upon the experience and closure. Certainly, not all of the theorists specify such a progression, but they acknowledge the value of each part, and probably would not object to placing them in a coherent order. Consider each part in turn.

One way to learn an agentic plot, whether for a dart game or for life, is through observing models with whom one can identify. To learn an agentic plot, one might study an agentic model. The model offers a holistic representation of what one is to become. As a holistic representation, a model is indefinitely analyzable. There is no way to come to an end. Rather, one can come to a deeper appreciation of or understanding of the whole. Much of what one learns is probably tacit, implicit rather than explicit (Polanyi 1967), requiring an empathic in-dwelling within the orientation and being of the model. However, a large part of the value of a model is that it is capable of inspiring a person, providing strong motivation to strive for more agency. The model is inspirational because it portrays a way, a path from the confines of what is to the possibilities of what might be.

Usually based upon models, imaginative rehearsal is holistic practice in taking an agentic role. When the inspiration of a model is powerful, imaginative rehearsal follows spontaneously, and it can take many forms (daydreaming, playacting or pretense, story-telling). In strong cases, a person might collect symbols (clothes, songs, etc.) and cultivate stylistic actions (a walk, phrase, manner-ism, etc.) that reflect the model. Through imaginative participa-tion, a person explores the possibilities of a model, masters some aspects of orientation, and composes a story line. Even if a model is not so moving as to stimulate imaginative rehearsals naturally, they can be deliberately guided.

The movement from imagination to actual enactment typi-cally requires some form of preparation. While the motivation to enact a certain way of being might be strong, one's capacity to do so is apt to be weak. Preparations might involve developing a skill, learning some area of knowledge, fortifying an attitude, develop-ing a repertoire of suitable and trustworthy responses, finding or shaping a setting, and the like. Preparatory exercises are not experi-enced as the "real" enactment, but they provide a bridge toward full and authentic enactments as well as providing partial actualizations of a way of being. Preparations can be both means and little ends in themselves.

Preparations culminate in action, which constitutes an enactment of an agentic orientation. It is not just a matter of successfully bringing something about, but of striving to bring something about in an agentic fashion, in a way that is an end in itself. An enactment is pervaded by the realities of a situation in which something is to be accomplished and by the ideals and imaginative possibilities of being an agent. Here, one is apt to be confronted with the difference between fantasy and genuine potential.

The very richness and significance of an enactment calls for reflection, a sizing up to bring the episode to closure. If the enactment is filled with discrepancies or is movingly successful, dwelling upon it is apt to be spontaneous. If seemingly uneventul, one can deliberately reflect upon it through discussion, among other things. The most basic task of reflection is to re-present and reexperience the enactment, weaving its elements into a story. Representing the experience offers the possibility of straightening the story, correcting deficits, smoothing the rough edges of an agentic posture, and thus, preparing for future enactments.

Generally, this sketch conforms with Kelly's (1955) cycle of personal construction (Neimeyer 1987), Heath's (1980) adaptive sequence, deCharms' (1976) personal causation program, and Cochran's (1986, 1990) view of a story, among others. What is gained from this outline of progression is that it embeds events within a plot in which their significance can be more clearly seen. For example, the sequence moves from spectator to participant, ending the cycle as a spectator. One builds on and prepares for the other. Difficulty in forming a model of agentic orientation is apt to impoverish and/or distort imaginative rehearsal. Difficulty in enacting an agentic orientation is apt to impoverish reflection. The significance of each phase depends upon its place in the plot, requiring attention to a balanced whole rather than overemphasis upon one phase to the neglect of others.

It is also worth noting that each phase is holistic. Certainly, one could emphasize parts (such as responsibility or skill), but as parts within a whole. The model is a whole. Imaginative rehearsal concerns a whole orientation. Preparations emphasize the significance of parts within a whole. And so on. At least from this preliminary attempt to make use of research studies of agency, it appears that enhancing agency is not a piecemeal building of parts, but a holistic effort from the start. Further, each phase can be regarded and experienced as a means and an end. Each phase is a means for enhancing agency and if done well, each is a constituent of what it means to be more of an agent. In part, this means that a person who went through the phases in a sheerly technological way, merely doing what one has to do to presumably improve, would go through them in the wrong way. As conceived here, each phase is intended to go somewhere, to be sure, but the best way to go somewhere is by taking delight or interest in each phase in itself.

Enough has been said in these preliminary comments to convey the general flavor of the sequence, enough to allow actual cases to elaborate or alter them. Now, let's turn to the kinds of experiences that are thought to enhance agency. These experiences include those concerned with self-determination, mastery, and challenge.

Self-determination

In a school program designed to enhance personal causation, deCharms (1976) emphasized four steps that were repeated. First, engage a person in self-study in order to identify meaningful motivations. Initially, self-study might be general, an attempt to identify strong motivations that seem enduring and pervasive. Then, self-study is narrowed to particular situations to identify meaningful bases for action in those situations. Second, a person is helped to translate motives into realistic but challenging goals. Third, a person plans and strives to reach goals, monitoring progress. Last, a person reflects on the experience, stressing one's responsibility for actions and consequences. These steps are then repeated for other enactments.

Preceding immersion in cycles of self-determined action, persons essentially learned a script for agency. For example, a person with strong personal causation (an origin) was described in contrast to someone with weak personal causation (a pawn). Students identified and discussed experiences from their own lives in which they felt like origins or pawns, being guided to an evaluation (e.g., is it better to be an origin?). A model of an origin was provided and discussed (i.e., Jesse Owens). Students then wrote stories to cultivate an agentic orientation. There are many ways to guide effective story writing. In this case, a vocabulary of agentic terms was developed for each story (e.g., striving, disappointment, goal, obstacle, means, etc.), and students incorporated these terms in their stories. In other programs, these stories might be examined to determine how they deviate from an agentic orientation. With this feedback, persons can revise their stories to more faithfully reflect agency. Last, games (e.g., a spelling contest) were designed to practice aspects of agency such as realistic but challenging goal setting. These activities took place within a warm, accepting atmosphere in which self-exploration was supported, and in which students could decide for themselves whether more agency was a self-improvement worth striving to attain.

Throughout the program, the quality of experience involved in self-determination—in being a personal cause—was prominent. In each cycle of enactment, students shaped achievable goals grounded in meaningful motivations. They planned and strove to reach those goals, noting how being a personal cause can make things happen and how they were thus responsible for actions and consequences. While these enactments incorporated most features of agency, they stressed the unique experience of being a causal agent in shaping one's world.

Mastery

Experiences of mastery are those that demonstrate one's capabilities for succeeding in a situation or task. Ordinarily, capacity involves knowledge and skill, but might include an indefinite number of other possibilities such as withstanding fear, maintaining concentration, or checking impulsivity. The theme of mastery punctuates outcome (success or failure) and an interpretation of what accounts for the outcome (e.g., effort, talent, chance, etc.). Successful demonstrations of mastery for which a person takes credit enhance confidence (self-efficacy, internal locus of control). Agency theorists (Adler 1956; Bandura 1989; Maddi 1988; Rotter 1966; White 1959) often seem to regard mastery experiences as the crucial vehicle for enhancing a sense of agency.

While self-determination and mastery are capable of being separated, each seems rather impotent without the other. For example, self-determination has little point if a person cannot use it to successfully create desired effects. Indeed, deCharms (1968) sometimes slips into talking of personal causation as mastery: "Man's primary motivational propensity is to be effective in producing changes in his environment" (p. 269). In contrast, success might be empty if a person does not believe it resulted from his or her own effort, choice, or sense of meaning. As a way to enhance agency, each experience only makes sense if the other is implicitly or explicitly assumed. Nevertheless, self-determination and mastery are often discussed as if the other did not exist or was of no importance.

Given the general sequence (model, imaginative rehearsal, etc.), a theme of mastery directs attention to effectiveness from beginning to end, and effectiveness is determined by whether or not one's capabilities were sufficient for success, assuming adequate effort. The model would show what a successful performance was like. In imaginative rehearsal, a person would envision himself or herself performing successfully. Preparations would test and develop capabilities for success. And following a successful enactment, reflection would emphasize an interpretation of success that favored one's capabilities. While this summary could be complicated considerably (e.g., factors that figure in attributing success to oneself), the basic plot for becoming more confident through successful experiences seems clear and generally sound.

Difficulties with mastery experiences stem largely from an imbalanced and overly restricted focus upon success. For example, a disproportionate emphasis upon outcome can reduce all preceding phases to means of no value in themselves, but only of value in forwarding an outcome. In this way, the intrinsic interest and value of models, preparations, and even the enactment might be undermined. Imbalanced by other features such as realism, one might claim credit for success and avoid blame for failure, leading to a false and probably brittle sense of agency that invites defensiveness. However, there is no reason why mastery experiences must be imbalanced or why interpretation must border on the ludicrous. The importance of mastery experiences remains, answering the question of whether a person can make a difference in his or her life.

Challenge

An intrinsically motivated activity is one that is done for its own sake. Certainly, an activity might be a means for other ends, but it is experienced as an end in itself. The mark of such an experience is enjoyment. Based on the research of Csikszentmihalyi (1975), an intrinsically motivated activity is pervaded by a sense of flow, of total involvement. "In the flow state, action follows upon action according to an internal logic that seems to need no conscious intervention by the actor. He experiences it as a unified flowing from one moment to the next, in which he is in control of his actions, and in which there is little distinction between self and environment, between stimulus and response, or between past, present, and future" (p. 36).

Typical characteristics of flow experience are loss of self-consciousness and loss of a sense of time (e.g., an hour might feel like a minute). One is immersed in the activity with no outside perspective, able to concentrate on the immediate task with little or no attention to other concerns, and feels in control of actions and the environment, effortlessly or with no conscious vigilance. Demands for action are coherent and feedback is clear and immediate.

According to Csikszentmihalyi (1975, 1990; M. Csikszentmihalyi and I. Csikszentmihalyi 1988), the fundamental condition for entering into flow is challenge. An activity is challenging if the demands of performance require a reasonably full use of skills. If little skill is required, one is more apt to be bored. If overmatched, a person is more apt to feel anxious or overwhelmed. Challenge requires a match between the demands of an activity and the skills (or capabilities generally) one has to meet those demands.

Challenge is also a core condition for agency theorists such as McClelland (1965), deCharms (1976), and Maddi (1988). Grounded in agency theories (e.g., White 1959), Deci (1975) conceived of intrinsically motivated activities as those in which a person seeks to exercise competence and self-determination. "People seem to be engaged in the general process of seeking and conquering challenges which are optimal for them" (p. 62). Trivial or excessive tasks yield boredom or fear, but in challenging tasks, a person seems to come alive as an agent, capable of intense satisfaction in an activity. In short, intrinsically motivated activities are those in which agency can be more fully exercised and in which a sense of agency can be more keenly experienced, and thus enhanced.

Csikszentmihalyi (1990), Deci (1975), and others have drawn out the developmental significance of challenging activities. Summarized most simply, a person must progress to stay challenged. One might begin learning chess, for instance, by playing other novices, but as one develops, playing novices would become boring. One must seek better opponents. In a related way, challenge leads on to more challenge. As a person develops more knowledge and skill, an activity opens up to greater variety and refinement. For example, chess opens up to a wide repertoire of offensive and defensive strategies, yielding delights that would be difficult to imagine for a beginner. As Deci has stressed, the progression required to maintain challenge provides a powerful vehicle for the differentiation of motives and interests.

Deci's cognitive model of behavioral cycles takes on the familiar form of the general sequence noted previously: stimulus, inputs, awareness of potential satisfaction (anticipatory arousal of motivation), goals and plans, goal-directed action, and satisfaction. For each step, there are various factors that might facilitate or hinder movement. However, of most importance here, Deci has argued and provided experimental support for the possibility that extrinsic rewards can undermine intrinsic motivation. The motivation to exercise competence and self-determination, to engage oneself in challenges is co-opted by the pursuit of rewards external to the activity, reducing the activity to but a means to a valued end. In this way, challenge stands in direct opposition to extreme versions of mastery experiences which overstress success or control of rewards. Sheerly instrumental activity simply highlights the wrong motivation for experiencing the agency-enhancing potency of challenge.

In summary, the three kinds of agentic experiences highlight somewhat different elements, but there seems to be no compelling reason why these elements would not fit together into one experience. For example, Kohn and Schooler (1983) found in a series of longitudinal studies that jobs which encourage occupational self-direction enhance self-direction generally, among other variables such as intellectual flexibility. Occupational self-direction is defined secondarily by lack of routinization in work, lack of close supervision, and primarily by the substantive complexity of tasks. Work that is substantively complex requires thought, independent judgment, personal initiative and discretion, and a fuller employment of knowledge and skill. Certainly, the conditions for occupational self-direction that have been described seem conducive to experiences of self-determination, mastery, and challenge, and as Kohn and Schooler's (1983) research demonstrates, cultivates a self-directed orientation in other spheres of life (leisure activities, parenting). While these experiences can be separated by over-emphasizing certain features and neglecting others, they also are capable of blending into one experience. From this perspective, to enhance a sense of agency is a matter of encouraging or guiding a person to engage in agentic experiences.

Toward a Narrative of Transformation

Thus far, the plot calls for steady progress as agentic experiences increase. There might be setbacks and problems to overcome (minimizing self-criticism, appraising reality more accurately or fruitfully, etc.), but the path of movement seems clear if one could but get firmly on it. While uncomplicated, the plot, such as it is, seems thin. The narrative context requires elaboration. Here, we are not so much concerned with the plot of a patient or agent, but with the narrative of how a person changes from one to the other.

In the beginning, the person is living the plot of a patient. In the end, the person is living the plot of an agent. A narrative of transformation in agency has a reasonably definite beginning and ending state, an opposition that bounds the line of movement. However, the middle seems problematic. In a transformation, a person is leaving one plot behind to arrive at an unfamiliar plot of living. Neither plot can serve as an adequate guide to the middle. If the plot of a patient served as a guide, one would still be stuck. If the plot of an agent served as a guide, one would already have achieved the end. The person is cast in between, relatively unscripted in the design of living. Since the middle is largely unplotted, disorientation is apt to be a prominent part of such a story, among other things. What seems necessary is to develop a narrative of transformation that can draw from plots of agency and patiency, but is neither. Transformation of this nature requires its own plot, distinct from that of a patient or agent.

A transformation from one way of being to another resembles the pattern of an initiation (Eliade 1958) or a rite of passage (Van Gennep 1960). Through examining rituals and ceremonies of life's crisis points (entering adulthood, birth, marriage, moving to a new location), Van Gennep was able to identify a common pattern across instances from diverse ages and cultures. This common story serves as a holistic model for understanding major themes of transformation, the significance of parts, and the plot as a whole. It provides a guide that might allow one to see what could easily be missed by focusing too narrowly upon agentic experiences.

Beginning

Beginning rituals emphasize separation from a way of being. The person is dislodged from a familiar status (e.g., child), removed from his or her customary setting, and secluded in a special dwelling or territory. For example, leaving the world of mother is separating from childhood. Mother and son might be informed that the child will be taken, killed by divine beings, and resurrected as an adult. It is a time of mourning for the mother and terror for the child. In one ceremony (Eliade 1958), mothers are covered with branches and blankets, not allowed to see or intervene. As youth sit waiting beside their mothers, they can hear bull-roarers sounding in the darkness and sticks beating on the ground. From the direction of the sacred ground, they can see burning sticks approaching. Suddenly, strangely dressed figures leap into the clearing, seize the youth, and take them off into the night. In one way or another, a youth is removed from the setting that supports a way of being.

Separation is thematically extended by diverse practices. For example, an initiate might be privileged with a tribal secret, but told that he will be killed if this secret is ever revealed to women and children (or men, as the case might be). However, the dominant way separation is initially extended is through death symbolism, dying to the old condition. Death symbols are pervasive in a rite of passage, beginning for instance with youth being taken into the darkness, the domain of childhood stories and nightmares.

In one scenario (Eliade, 1958), youth are told they must die and are made to stay in a house full of ants until they are badly bitten. Then, they are taken to a "death cabin" where they live without any clothes and in complete solitude. Often, a special dwelling is called the belly of the monster, in which one is "digested" by a monster or divine being to be resuscitated later. In another scenario, youth observe a man go into a tunnel or deep ditch in which he is presumably attacked by divine beings. After some commotion, the man comes out of the tunnel, apparently exhausted and badly wounded (blood all over him). Now, the youth are ordered into the tunnel, one by one. Other practices include going without sleep, beatings, and mutilation (e.g., removing a tooth), all experienced as analogous to dying.

In the logic of a rite of passage, following Eliade (1958), to be reborn as a higher and different order of being, one must first die to the lower order of being. Dying is equivalent to being born. In the context of a transformation of agency, this logic indicates that the effects of agentic experiences are not impressed upon a neutral human nature, a blank slate, but upon a person who is already attached to and immersed within an ongoing way of being as a patient. Attached, a person is apt to be reluctant to let go of the familiar with its own unfinished business and satisfactions. Submerged, to use a term from Freire (1982), the person is apt to lack the perspective to generate a viable alternative. The practices of separation seem uniquely designed to enable a person to detach and emerge from a way of living, to experience detachment and emergence.

Social Ceremonies

Agentic experiences as portrayed tend to be isolated, lacking a social context. Rites of passage provide a vivid reminder of the power of social ceremonies. Garfinkel's (1956) conditions for degradation ceremonies seem as good a way as any, for instance, to encage a person as a patient. In a degradation ceremony, a person is transformed from one public identity to a lower, more degraded kind of person. From the perspective of other people, the person is recast, reinterpreted, becoming essentially a different and lower person. From the individual's perspective, he or she is also recast and reinterpreted, perhaps not as absolutely, but enough to engender guilt and shame, self-disgust. The person would like to run and hide, slink away, shrivel to invisibility, and the like. The scenario begins with a denouncer, witnesses to the denunciation, and the accused with his or her deed.

In summary, acting as a public representative (not from personal motives), the denouncer must be invested with the authority to speak of ultimate values, to be a supporter of those values, and to make these values salient as a reason for denunciation. There is a distance between the denouncer and the accused. In the denunciation, the accused and his or her deed are made to stand out as extraordinary, removed from the routine and customary. The deed is elevated to a negative type that reflects the undesirable bent of the accused, standing in stark contrast to the sacred, positive type (e.g., criminal versus honest citizen). Last, the accused or denounced person is ritually removed from his or her place in the legitimate order, made to seem strange, outside, or opposed to the social order and its value orientation. Essentially, the person must be seen as cast out because of his or her flawed or perverted character, which now serves to define the person in contrast to what is good or right.

Numerous experiences in everyday life meet all or most of Garfinkel's conditions. As one example, getting fired or demoted can approximate a degradation ceremony, or perhaps offer a variant of such a ceremony (e.g., people might feel upended by betrayal, disillusioned more than ashamed). In one layoff, employees to be terminated were segregated in a meeting room. After being informed of their termination, security guards escorted each person to his or her desk for personal items, and then escorted them out (Avasthi 1990). In a two-year longitudinal study, Andrisani and Nestel (1976) found that males who were promoted increased in an internal locus of control while males who were demoted decreased. Perhaps other factors contributed to this charge such as challenging work. However, it also seems likely that the upgrading or degrading nature of these experiences contributed to the change.

In any case, rites of passage emphasize the social context of experiences, the regard of others, and the establishment of status.

In ordinary life, we commonly experience being "built up" or "put down" (in education, marriage, contacts with institutions, informal gatherings, and so on). While most experiences are apt to be transient in effect, there are others that are so frequent or powerful that a sense of agency might be enhanced or undermined.

End

The end of a rite of passage is the opposite of the beginning. A person is reincorporated back into the tribe or group. Through ceremonies that highlight belonging and a new status, a person is included back into his or her once familiar setting. Ceremonies of incorporation commonly involve feasts (Van Gennep 1960). Legitimation of a new and higher status commonly involves the exercise of role actions that are sanctioned only for members of the higher group. With the acceptance and approval of the tribe or group, those who have completed the passage begin adjusting to a new way of living, careful to maintain in their attitudes and conduct the ideals of their new roles.

Middle

During the transitional period, the person wavers between two ways or worlds. Over the first half, a person is subjected to experiences that are painful, tiring (mentally and physically), and terrifying, all thematically unified as dying to the old condition. Over the second half, a person is given special instruction and a name, allowed participation in sacred ceremonies, and generally introduced to uplifting experiences and deeper understandings, all thematically unified as being born to a new condition. While the middle gradually shifts from destruction to construction, the dominant cycle of dying and being born seems to pervade experiences throughout the middle. Over the course of transition, elements of dying decline in intensity and frequency, while elements of being born increase. The beginning and end but punctuate what is an indefinite series of such experiences as trial and preparation, tearing down and building up.

The middle is filled with tortures (e.g., beatings), mutilations (e.g., circumcision), ordeals (long hikes), vigils (going without sleep), prohibitions and taboos, revelations, participation (in songs, ceremonies, etc.), and role enactments (e.g., acting like a ghost or baby). Van Gennep (1960) argued that these practices are intended to progressively weaken and then reshape the personality. Eliade (1958) has indicated the value of many scenarios, their role in moving a transition story along. For example, removing a tooth makes youth identical to adults of the tribe. Prohibitions constitute ascetic exercises that force initiates to concentrate or meditate (e.g., restricting vision to only the ground between one's feet). Physical ordeals and terrifying scenes open the novice to other and higher values while showing the inadequacy of his or her more childish disposition. Aside from general functions, the way each part of a rite of passage is conducted and symbolized has a particular meaning within a culture. Each has significance for the mythological traditions and practices of the tribe, and in this sense, each part eventually becomes revelatory.

While the middle facilitates dying to one condition in order to be reborn to another condition, it has a distinctive character of its own, quite apart from the thematic emphases of beginning and end. That is, the middle fulfills the basic logic of a transitional plot. To reattach to a higher way of living, one must first detach from a lower way of living. To become oriented as an agent, one must separate from the orientation of a patient. However, change takes time and in the middle, one lives detachment and disorientation. A person is suspended between two orientations, neither one nor the other. Transition emphasizes uncertainty, ambivalence, ambiguity, restlessness, withdrawal, instability, confusion, moodiness, and the like. As aptly portrayed in rites of passage, one is ghost-like, insubstantial, unanchored, a novice in life. Such a condition is ideal for exploring, searching, reflecting, experimenting, and imagining.

Without a council of elders to guide a transition, a transformation in agency seems similar to the creativity cycle described by Ghiselin (1955). At the beginning and during much of the middle, the end is not in sight. One strives for more agency in living, but a coherent and compatible conception or image of an agent is as yet unformed, leaving a person to pursue, elaborate, and eventually piece together fragments. Following Ghiselin, the middle would be composed of alternating periods of conscious and unconscious activity. During conscious periods of deliberate effort, a person might develop a skill, gather information, try out a role (or roles), seek models, discuss possibilities, cultivate an interest, and the like. Deliberate effort sensitizes and equips a person for spontaneous and creative productions. Unconscious activity or incubation might yield insights, revelations, novel possibilities, and eventually a holistic vision of what it is to be an agent of one's own life. Products of incubation are checked, polished, adopted or abandoned in the next phase of deliberate effort.

From this perspective, the plot of a transition is a search for something one cannot clearly specify. In retrospect, the interweaving themes of dying to patiency and being born to agency might be dominant, but the experience of the middle is more apt to be "tension and tendency . . . a working sea of indecision . . . commerce with disorder" (Ghiselin 1955, p. 14). It is this plunge into disorder that allows a new order to be formed. As Ghiselin has noted, to endure disorientation in a productive way requires special virtues such as discipline, industry, patience, dedication, and wholeheartedness, and these virtues are precisely those that are often mentioned in relation to the scenarios of a rite of passage (Eliade 1958).

Identity and Agency

In becoming an agent, a person constructs a different configuration of meaning to live. In becoming an agent of one's career or course of life, that configuration of meaning concerns a life story. Or more precisely, a person adopts a particular role in a drama of life (McAdams 1985; MacIntyre 1984; Polkinghorne 1988). This life story has been variously referred to as a style of life (Adler 1956), a life theme (Csikszentmihalyi and Beattie 1979), or a fundamental project (Sartre 1966; Charme 1984).

> The experience of self is organized along the temporal dimension in the same manner that the events of a narrative are organized by the plot into a unified story. The self is that temporal order of human existence whose story

begins at birth, has as its middle the episodes of a lifespan, and ends with death. It is the plot that gathers together these events into a coherent and meaningful unity, and thereby gives context and significance to the contribution that the individual episodes make toward the overall configuration that is the person. The whole of an individual human existence is articulated in the narrative plot; it is much more than a a simple chronicle listing of life occurrences. The self, then, is a meaning rather than a substance or a thing. To look for it in the objective plane is to make a mistake similar to that of examining the substance of the ink on a piece of paper in order to find the meaning of the word it prints. (Polkinghorne 1988, p. 152)

John Stuart Mill (1969) was a reformer of opinions and institutions. Booker T. Washington (1956) was an uplifter of the trapped and downtrodden to a place of constructive participation in society. Lincoln Steffens (1931) was a muckraker who investigated and reported the corrupt underside of social institutions in order to stimulate improvement. Their entire lives were bound up in a coherent narrative of how they became what they were and what followed. For example, as a slave before emancipation, Washington's early recollections involve many instances of being trapped. In contrast, education symbolized a way out of life's traps, a vehicle for taking one as far as one's determination and capability would allow. In helping others, Washington sought to uplift people from bleak confinement just as he had been uplifted. Life plots vary considerably, but in successful cases, each weaves the succession of events into a temporal whole, making life a sustained action rather than a disjointed series of disparate actions.

Becoming an agent in one's career or life story is closely bound to forming an identity (Erikson 1959). For example, Washington could not adopt the identity of an uplifter without feeling adequate for the part, without a sense of agency as an uplifter. Reformer, muckraker, and uplifter require a sense of agency as part of what each means as a character in a particular drama. This does not suggest that Washington, for instance, did not experience a lack of confidence at times, or question his fundamental evaluations. Struggle is part of the story and no unrealistic requirements would be desired. It does assert, however, that if Washington lacked confidence (or other agentic features) in a more enduring way, if he could not really believe in the possibility of being an uplifter, then he could not adopt such an identity with any authenticity.

The reason why this is so is that identity is not a separate thing to which one might add agentic attributes. Rather, lacking certain meanings of agency, an identity becomes a different kind of identity. For example, a reformer might become a deformer, or simple bungler. In Cochran's (1990) investigation of lives, each person formed an identity amid threats or spoiled forms of that identity. As one instance, Steffens (1931) was threatened by the image of a colleague who was a cynical, run-down drunk. Apparently, this person's investigative reporting had been so disillusioning that it undermined any hope or positive belief. In Steffen's autobiography, this man served as a warning, the ghost of Steffens' future, that he strove to avoid. Because a sense of agency figures in the meaning of an identity, it is required to maintain that identity and there are always, it seems, numerous threats that portray deviant and sometimes devastating story lines, should one stray off course.

A sense of agency is separate from identity in a different way. Identity is a broader term and a person could form an identity in which patiency or a lack of agency was salient. For example, a person might form an identity as a victim. For this reason, we can claim that a sense of agency figures in identity, but cannot specify any absolute or uniform relation. What is required depends upon the nature of the identity formed, the character in a life story. Even agentic identities might require different aspects of agency, emphasizing some features and not others. For example, in his life as an adventurer, Casanova (1984) minimized planfulness. "I never had any fixed aim before my eyes, and that my system, if it can be called a system, has been to glide away unconcernedly on the stream of life, trusting to the wind wherever it led . . . My errors . . . will teach . . . the great art of treading on the brink of the precipice without falling into it" (p. 1). However, it might be more correct to claim that he minimized planning over longer courses for his scheming in the moment was usually lavish and detailed, albeit often spontaneous. Nevertheless, planfulness for Casanova was very different than it was for Mill, Washington, or Steffens, playing a different role in the ongoing narration of a life course.

That a particular identity involves relatively unique role demands, style, and tasks seems evident and in no need of further description here, although it will be of considerable importance in examining actual cases since a plot of life locates a sense of agency, gives it bounds and definition. What is worthy of note here is that the problems and paths of identity formation become directly relevant to becoming an agent of one's life story. Enhancing a sense of agency takes place in the context of becoming an uplifter, a reformer, a muckraker, an adventurer, or whatever.

If the narrative form of a rite of passage provides the general plot for enhancing agency, issues of identity provide the content. And the content can shape the plot further, perhaps in relatively unique ways. At stake is a redramatization of one's life course, clarifying a narrative that encompasses a life and makes it more livable (more meaningful, fulfilling, or productive), shaping a role in this story (role ideals, capabilities, demands, etc.), defining essential tasks of a project, and populating this dramatic definition of life with other roles or characters with whom one is aligned or opposed. A transformation of agency is a sweeping attempt to reauthor a life. While this connection between agency and identity complicates matters considerably, expanding what is at stake and what must be considered, it seems unavoidable. A sense of agency is a configuration of meaning that features in a larger composition of meaning, taking on the problems and issues of the context in which it figures.

Actualization of Meaning

As yet, there is no principle of order that could account for a transformation in a sense of agency. The problem is that a person is unguided in a transitional story. In perhaps most experiences of life, a person is implicitly or explicitly guided by a plot. For example, Steffens (1931) enacted the plot of a muckraking reporter for most of his life. Somewhat like a musical composition accounts for diverse performances of it, a prior plot accounts for enactments. However, in a transitional story, the person is unplotted, as it were. The pattern of a rite of passage is not really a plot that a person follows, but a plot that makes intelligible a period of life after it has happened. It offers a third-person perspective rather than the first-person perspective of the main character. While such a plot might help in understanding a transformation in agency, it does not credibly account for how the change came about. We lack a principle for how people are guided to fulfill a coherent pattern when they are unguided by a plot or by a preestablished series of social ceremonies.

From another perspective, what we have so far are a number of parts that are apt to fit into a story of transformation. There are various cycles of experience (participant and spectator, reason and intuition as in a creativity cycle) and types of experiences (status enhancement and degradation, self-determination, mastery, challenge). These cycles and types of experiences fulfill various functions in redramatizing the world. They help to compose one story line and decompose another, to provide inspiration for a new role in a life story, and to foster mastery of that role. However, it seems clear that experiences might stimulate random, arbitrary, or disorderly movements that do not cohere into a transition story. What is capable of rendering a coherent whole from the potential of a disorderly collection of parts? What is capable of giving the transition a non-arbitrary character?

Once started, a transformation from a patient to an agent in a life course is governed by the Gestalt Law of Pregnance (Fuller 1990). The beginning might well be arbitrary or just a matter of good fortune. For example, a serious accident might remove a person from one story of life to search for another. Becoming frustrated with being a patient in life, a person might do something that allows one to gain distance and glimpse other possibilities. Whatever the case, the beginning serves to dislodge a person, at least partially, from one story line and to place a person on another story line that is as yet vague. The Law of Pregnance does not account for the beginning, but operates to fulfill or actualize embryonic meanings that are glimpsed in the beginning. In the beginning, a person is confronted with a dramatic construction that is flawed, vague, imbalanced, unrefined, or unelaborated. As a drama one lives, it is off, not right, or in short, a flawed whole. In this context, the Law of Pregnance is that a lived drama will change toward becoming as good a drama as possible, given limitations and impediments of oneself, others, and circumstances.

As one example, consider a short period from the life of Lincoln Steffens (1931). In early life, Steffens was given to an overly idealized view of the world with good winning over evil through the determined efforts of good people. Cut from the same bark as heroes, Steffens envisioned himself with a heroic stature. He imagined and playacted heroic roles over and over. Toward the end of childhood and throughout adolescence, Steffens endured a long series of disillusioning experiences. He discovered that adults lied, that horse races were fixed, that state government was a sham, a show for suckers, and so on. Nothing was as it seemed and his idealized world was simply not real. While he knew that his idealized vision of things was untrue, he did not know what was true. He developed a dramatic cast of characters such as suckers (those who took things as they seemed), those in the know, front men, bosses behind the scene, and developed a vocabulary for defining situations such as show, sham, and the like. In this emerging drama, the good people tended to be suckers while the bad people were behind the scenes and knew how things really worked. He had no place to stand. While aligned with good people, he did not want to be a sucker. On the other hand, he was opposed to bad people. Steffens was cast in between with no authentic role he could avow.

In the years preceding his entrance to university, his position became more precarious. The early dream that he was destined to be a great man still lingered, and Steffens postured excessively in transient roles that were soon undermined. When he had to ride seven miles to get a doctor for a sick woman, he was horrified at himself for making a needed task into a chance to be heroic. "Mrs. Neely was really ill, needed me, and- and- this is what hurt: I had been glad she was sick so that I could make an unselfish dash to town for the doctor . . . I was like the rest of the world; I was not what I seemed. I was a sham. And I didn't want to be a sham. No, I didn't" (pp. 79–80). In another episode, Steffens got into trouble at a private school, for drinking and leading other boys into a drunken celebration. It was another pose, as his father told him: "All that worries me is your posings, the bunk you have seemed always to like. I never saw you do anything for the fun of doing it; you always wanted to tell about it and see yourself and be seen doing it" (p. 109). Steffens was becoming disillusioned with himself, his idealistic compulsion to pose as a hero; it was all sham. Yet posing was nearly all he had at the time; he had no real position to act from.

Yearning to go to university, to find answers to the questions that bothered him, Steffens was stalled a year until he could pass qualifying examinations. During this time, he was enrolled in a private school, where he was inspired by his teacher, Evelyn Nixon. Nixon claimed he was nobody, just a seeker of knowledge and one who could appreciate the good works of others. Nixon refused to answer young Steffens' questions, roaring at him that everything remains to be done. Nothing has been finally answered or completed. That was the task of youth, to answer those questions that older generations could not. Nixon inspired Steffens not to become heroic, but scholarly. Steffens yearned to know, not to be or do, but the way of being as a scholar was vividly impressed upon him during evening discussions of the faculty which he was allowed to attend.

In these discussions, nothing was ever concluded. Brilliantly and eloquently, evidence was offered, the testimony of wise persons was presented, but no conclusion was reached. Questions were left open, and indeed, expanded, fueling Steffens' yearning for answers. "My head, busy with questions before, was filled with holes that were aching voids as hungry, as painful, as an empty stomach. And my questions were explicit; it was as if I were not only hungry; I was hungry for certain foods. My curiosity was no longer vague" (p. 115). Rather than fill those hungers, the discussions generated new ones by a sophisticated cultivation of ignorance, a survey of unsolved problems. Why did people not know how to love? Why could people not govern themselves effectively? Overwhelmed with the knowledge of these men (who could quote a Papal Bull in the original Latin or recite relevant verses and paragraphs of great authors), these discussions left Steffens afire with questions rather than answers.

However, what impressed Steffens the most was their objectivity, what he called their scientific attitude. In discussing questions, they set themselves aside. They were more interested in the world than in themselves, able to approach topics without any apparent self-interest. The topics were bigger than their egos, so it seemed to Steffens, allowing them to be impersonal and detached in their deliberations. Being a nobody, as his teacher phrased it, was becoming increasingly defined as a quite definite type of person, one that was incompatible with egocentric posturing.

Over and over in growing up, Steffens had entered experiences with enthusiastic idealism and left in disillusionment, agonizing questions. Now as a young man in university, he quite deliberately sought disillusionment. Disillusioning himself had become equivalent to penetrating through the show to social reality, yet he lacked any sound or systematic method of investigation. In an American History course, he found himself developing just such a method, spurred on by his desire to know and with some help from his professor. Initially, he generated mystery by dwelling on different sources, noting how they differed on opinion and fact. He then expanded the search to other authorities, noting further discrepancies and developing further questions. Eventually, he worked his way back to original documents or some other solid basis, initiating a fresh search of fundamental grounds, trying to piece together a valid account. He was exhilarated by what he was discovering and the sheer excitement of investigation. As he investigated, the world opened up as a vast unknown with endlessly rich possibilities to pursue. "Nothing is done. Everything in the world remains to be done or done over" (p. 126).

Perhaps ironically, this lack of a firm foundation, of answers, provided part of an answer to one of Steffens' enduring and agonizing questions. "I was stunned by the discovery that . . . nothing is known; that it is precisely the foundation that is lacking for science; that all we call knowledge rested upon assumptions which the scientists did not all accept; and that, likewise there is no scientific reason for saying, for example, that stealing is wrong. In brief: there was no scientific basis for ethics. No wonder men said one thing and did another; no wonder they could settle nothing in life or in the academies" (p. 127).

For the sake of brevity, many strands of theme and experience have been left out, but hopefully enough has been conveyed to capture the flow of development. In this summary, Steffens began enduring disillusionment and ended with disillusionment or investigation as a purpose. He began with no role in life, yet with many poses, and ended with an initial shaping of a role he could avow. In the beginning of this summary, Steffens felt impotent in his disillusionment. In the end, he was starting to feel a strengthening of agency in investigation, which was to eventually become his life work. Now, how did this change come about?

Most of the ingredients discussed in this chapter are clearly evident in this account. Separation from the old story involved Steffens' growing alienation from an idealistic picture of the world and the posture of a hero. Incorporation of a new story was evident. His investigation was a powerful agentic experience. There were models, imaginative rehearsals, preparations, and the like. However, our question is not so much concerned here with the importance of these parts as with understanding the flow of development as a holistic, nonarbitrary movement.

From an objective viewpoint, there is a great deal of chance and contingency in the narrative. For example, what is the likelihood that a person would get a chance to play the hero in a drama of rescue, would encounter a model, or would have the opportunity to participate in a significant social ceremony like a faculty discussion. More farfetched still, what is the probability that Steffens would experience the various parts in a flowing order at precisely the times he needed them to move forward? If we are restricted to the traditional view that an objective event produces a personal effect (e.g., observing an agentic model enhances, say, self-efficacy), then what happened to Steffens is a string of coincidences, of good fortune. On the other hand, it might be argued that this viewpoint is too impoverished and inadequate to account for a holistic flow of development. Outside of very simple laboratory experiments, it simply does not work very well. That is, it would require us to deny and ignore the numerous accounts that are just as flowing as Steffens', reducing them all to improbable coincidences (clarity in particular, fuzziness or blindness to the whole in which particulars figure).

From a more constructivist viewpoint, a person is shaping as well as being shaped. The major vehicle for shaping is plot or dramatic form. A bad plot or gestalt is restless, to use Fuller's (1990) term, in need of further shaping. Something more is required and that requiredness involves "the rightness of direction of a meaning" (Fuller 1990, p. 118). A gestalt is bad if its parts do not fit together well or parts are absent, good if parts crystallize together into a balanced, clear, and simple form. In this way, the Law of Pregnance is concerned with the actualization of meaning. In this study, actualization of meaning concerns the elaboration of a life plot.

Consider, for instance, the significance of Steffens' teacher as a model of scholarly objectivity. As an obvious fact, Steffens had been exposed to potential models for years. Everyone he met was a possible model, yet he responded so strikingly to Nixon because the meaning this teacher personified was required to fill out the drama he was then living. First, he was suspended without a viable role for participation in the world, restless, searching, and in short, in a high state of readiness to seize just such an opportunity as Nixon and his colleagues presented. Second, he was worn out with heroism, becoming increasingly alienated from his posturings, but the alternative of being a nobody lacked definition or lacked any desirable definition. Third, he was already embarked on a new plot, yearning to have his burning questions answered (by professors, no doubt), but this plot was embryonic and lacked an active role. For these reasons, among others, clarifying a role was required to develop his plot line further. Meeting this teacher and participating in those uplifting discussions might well be regarded as good fortune, but the actualization of meaning is non-arbitrary. If it were not Nixon who stimulated a dramatic development, it would eventually have been someone else.

Now, a role such as objective scientist, investigator, or one who formulates questions and pursues answers must also be filled out in the requiredness of its meaning. Most obviously, an investigator ought to know how to investigate, and that is the significance of his class project that crystallized an approach to historical investigation. It was tremendously empowering, moving Steffens to great enthusiasm. The strands of a life that come together in a life story are truly startling, suggesting the utter complexity of the task. For example, the seemingly small shift from being disillusioned to seeking disillusionment was pivotal in his life history, leading to a configuring of meaning in the activity of investigation. That these strands come together so eloquently in lives cannot be accounted for by any resort to chance or piecemeal building blocks. Rather, the development of an agentic life plot is guided, and this guidance is what is offered by the Law of Pregnance, as applied to plot. A lived plot will move toward as good a plot form as possible, given the circumstances. Or, a lived plot will move toward an increasing actualization of meaning, directed by what is required in the necessity of its own scheme of meaning.

About this movement, two comments seem noteworthy. First, during a transition, a person is guided toward a good gestalt or plot by the imperfections of the plot being lived at the time, but the person is apt to feel unguided, groping, searching, puzzling, and exploring. Guidance, such as it is, is not explicit or at least never fully explicit. The solutions to Steffens' difficulties in living were not there for conscious examination. Consciously, Steffens focused upon one highlighted part after another (e.g., going to university to get answers from professors). These explicit figures that guide conscious striving emerge from (if all is going well) a tacit ground that is not fully open to conscious efforts. Guidance from this tacit ground of a holistic plot-in-formation is open more to intuitive processes (urges, feelings, dreams, and daydreams). Potentially, guided fantasy might be an effective strategy for revealing the larger plot.

Second, experiences that constitute a significant plot development vary in the degree to which they can be specified. Retrospectively, in cases such as Steffens, dramatic development appears so flowing with uncanny precision as to be inevitable. Such is not the case. The requiredness of meaning at a time depends upon the developmental state of the plot. In a highly developed plot, perhaps what is required would be precise. However, in plots that are not so highly developed (as in a transition), what is required might be more general and flexible. All that might be required is resonance in meaning with the themes of a story line. For example, while the stance of an objective "nobody" might seem required, providing the outline of a positive role and separating from the heroic and ideal, it could have been otherwise. Suppose that Steffens had been befriended and charmed by, for example, a political boss behind the scenes who could answer questions and offer a position of one in the know. As matter of fact, Steffens later found these "bosses" to be gifted, attractive individuals, very far from any stereotype of evil villains. Might such a person have offered a model of a hidden hero? Of course, it is difficult to determine at this point, and speculative in any case, but the possibility seems open that Steffens could have developed somewhat differently, crystallizing the material of his life in another way that appeared in retrospect to be inevitable.

The Need for Case Studies

According to Yin (1984), case study research "allows an investigation to retain the holistic and meaningful characteristics of real-life events" (p. 14). In the present investigation, a case study provides a detailed, narrative description of how a person changed from a patient to an agent in living, portraying the events and influences that made such a transformation possible. Each case represents a concrete model of transformation in agency, embodied in the particulars of an individual life. For the topic of this book, case study has three distinct advantages.

First, in a case study, one need not worry about applicability to life. As contrived, often artificial, and very simple tasks, experiments might be questioned as to relevance to life outside the laboratory. For example, in days gone by, what did memorizing nonsense syllables really have to do with learning? Experimentally, there seems always to be a gap between a controlled laboratory procedure and applicability to a topic as related to everyday life. By contrast, there is no gap of this kind for a case study.

Second, narrative accounts of transformation can be compared to narrative expectations based on theory and research. For example, do case study descriptions of change resemble the transition plot of a rite of passage? Does the constructive half of the plot involve a series of agentic experiences? Is there evidence for the actualization of meaning toward a good gestalt? In this chapter and the previous one, several cycles (e.g., participant to spectator), functions (mastering a role), and complex issues (the peculiarities of authorship) were presented. Are they represented in concrete accounts? There are also several questions such as whether agency is bound by a role identity in a life plot that can be investigated in case studies. When research questions involve complex patterns (in contrast to rather simple hypotheses), a concrete pattern such as a case study provides an advantageous approach for examining adequacy.

Third, in addition to matching patterns from case studies with patterns based on theory and research, the case studies can be compared with one another. That is, we are interested in a transformation from a patient to an agent in living. We have ten detailed descriptions of how individuals actually made such a change. Given these ten concrete models of transformation, are there extensive commonalities? Might we be able to develop an abstract plot of the change that is faithful to each individual account? This advantage is largely exploratory, an attempt to discover patterns or refinements of patterns that are not present in current theory or research.

To avoid a lengthy detour, the method will only be summarized here. Through Joan's network of contacts, twenty-five people were referred, from which ten individuals were selected to participate in the study, five men and five women ranging in age from twenty-eight to sixty-four. First, each participant took part in a screening interview in which each person provided three short stories of the way he or she was before the change and three short stories portraying oneself after the change. These stories were scored according to deCharms' (1976) coding system for thought samples. Out of a possible eighteen points for three stories (six points per story), the "before" stories ranged from scores of one to six points. "After" stories ranged from thirteen to eighteen points, indicating substantial change.

Second, a lengthier interview was conducted to gain a description of the change. To help participants order their account and refresh their memories, a chronology of change was initially elicited. Using a line drawn across a sheet of paper with endpoints labeled beginning and end, each participant placed landmark events on the line to outline the change. Participants listed from eight to fifteen events, briefly describing each. After this preliminary organization and warm-up was complete, participants used these change lines in describing the transformation in as much detail as possible. Participants were cued by questions (How did it begin? What happened in the middle? How did it end?) and provided with a full orientation to the study. During the interview, Joan (who conducted all interviews) used basic counseling skills such as paraphrasing, requesting clarification or elaboration, and some empathic responses. Primarily, however, she tried to be fully present to each participant's description, creating a meaningful dialogue.

Third, using a fifty-two-item Q-sort (Stephenson 1953) that was specifically designed for this study, each participant Q-sorted each of his or her landmark events. The fifty-two items were drawn from major theories of agency. Participants sorted the items into nine groups, ranging from most characteristic of a particular event to least characteristic. In this way, theoretically significant concepts or phrases were used to describe each event. In a Q-sort, each item is scored upon the basis of the pile into which it was put. With nine piles, scores for items ranged from nine (most characteristic) to one (least characteristic). If a participant had mentioned eight landmark events, for instance, Q-sorting resulted in an eight by fifty-two matrix of scores. Completing these Q-sorts took one or more separate interviews.

Each matrix (for all ten participants) was subjected to an unrotated principal component analysis that yielded event loadings on each component and Z scores for items on each component. The event loadings for the first three components were graphed for a quantitative picture of the transformation. Item scores were used to describe the change.

Once the Q-sort data were analyzed, Joan returned to each participant for an elaboration interview. Participants were told that the Q-sort results provided indications of how the transformation in agency occurred, but required personal elaboration of meaning to be understood. While participants were encouraged to question, confirm, or qualify the results, the aim of the interview was not so much confirmation, but an attempt to stimulate a further elaboration of meaning. Results were presented in the form of two kinds of probes, a content probe and a pattern probe.

A content probe was formed by examining the first component, the pattern of change in event loadings. Item scores exceeding 1.5 or less than -1.5 were used to define the change. Below is one example. After the probe was given, Joan paused to allow the participant to respond, and then using reflection and empathic responses, encouraged the person to dwell upon and elaborate the meaning of the results.

> Let's take what seems to be the main component of change. You descended into a trap in which you accepted the influence and goals of others, holding them more or less responsible, yet felt anxious, depressed, and worthless. It was not a satisfying situation. Toward the end, you achieved a freedom from others' influence, a sense of optimism, worth, and satisfaction as you became your own person rather than engulfed by others.

A pattern probe was formed by examining the graph of the component that most defined the change. Hypothetically, change in event loadings might reflect gradual improvement, sudden improvement, or up and down cycles until the person levels off as a more potent agent. Below is an example of a pattern probe that was accompanied by a graphic representation of the change.

> This movement of freedom from the engulfment of others shows extreme cycles of change, soaring improvement and devastating setbacks before you levelled off as a freer, more optimistic person.

A content and pattern probe were presented for the second principal component. Then, an attempt was made to integrate both components into an overall thematic statement of change, as illustrated below.

> The main theme of change, according to Q-sort results, seems to be this. If a person can continue to act responsibly and determinedly, even when feeling trapped and dominated by others, and when one is most weak (feeling worthless, depressed, and lacking a sense of meaning), one will eventually gain a sense of freedom and optimism, worth and satisfaction.

Fourth, based upon the Q-sort results and transcriptions of all interviews (each was tape-recorded), we collaborated on the writing of a narrative description for each participant. As much as possible, we used the participants' own words or phrases, trying to maintain their perspective and sense of meaning on the change. Particular attention was also directed to the beginning and end, and the sequence of experiences that made up the middle. These accounts were written and revised until both of us agreed that each reflected the quantitative and qualitative evidence.

Last, each narrative description was further validated in two ways. In the first way, an independent reviewer (all had or were completing a doctorate in counseling psychology) studied an account and checked it against tapes of interviews and transcriptions. They were asked to search for and comment on any distortions, inaccuracies, or significant omissions. They also were asked to judge whether the interviews were unbiased, noting any instances of leading questions or inappropriate influence. In the second way, accounts were returned to participants to review their own stories of transformation. In a final interview, each was asked whether the account accurately portrayed his or her experience and whether anything of significance was left out. Occasionally, accounts were also reviewed by someone who was close to the person during the transformation.

The independent reviews were uniformly positive with occasional comments worth consideration. For example, in one account, the reviewer noted that the enthusiasm with which the participant spoke was not fully captured in written form. The participant self-reviews were also uniformly positive with more clarifications or corrections of small points and some subtle adjustments. In most cases, the participant was strongly moved by reading the account and dwelled on it for days or weeks after the interview. Many initiated phone calls to discuss points further. Given these two forms of review and collaborative agreement, the narrative descriptions appear to be a faithful reflection of participants' construction of the transformation.

3 / PHASES OF TRANSFORMATION

The aim of this chapter is to present the common pattern of transformation that is evident in the various case studies. To illustrate this pattern, or regular movement from one phase to another, two cases of serious injury are reported, largely because recovery from physical disability has the advantage of making more features of change reasonably clear and explicit. Injury casts a person in the role of a patient. When injury is serious, resulting in permanent disability, one is threatened with the prospect of becoming a chronic patient. The threat is so forceful, direct, and engulfing that rehabilitation becomes largely a struggle to become an agent once more, capable of shaping one's life (Wright 1983). The life one had before the accident is over and one must now strive to recover a life worth living.

Ray's Narrative

At the time of the interviews, Ray was thirty-two years old, married with one child. He grew up in a middle-class family, the oldest of four children. During childhood, the family moved several times before settling in a small town. At the age fifteen, he was regarded as a promising athlete. He loved sport and outdoor recreation. His life was changed by a car accident that left him paralyzed in both legs. After physical rehabilitation, he completed high school and earned a bachelor's degree in physical education. Ray is currently working on behalf of disabled people in universities.

Ray's memory of the accident is vivid, like a slow motion action sequence in a movie. Shortly before on that beautiful summer day, life had seemed so precious. He loved outdoor recreation, was devoted to sport, and was becoming interested in girls. He had control of his life and that life seemed very good, even though his parents had difficulty in getting along with one another. After the accident, he felt as though he had lost control. His legs would not work. One physician said he would never walk again. Another said that there was hope. Pain kept him centered on the immediate moment, struggling to stay on top of it. He was unable or perhaps unprepared to think too far ahead.

When the operation on his back was finally done, he had plenty of time. For one and a half months, he could not move. Every three hours if the nurses remembered, he was rotated from front to back or vice versa. As each day of inactivity passed with no improvement, Ray settled into despair and felt depressed a lot of the time. He hung on, hoping for recovery, resolving himself to uncertainty, focusing on one day at a time. Every day for hours, he willed his legs to move, but they never did.

As replayed over and over, the accident became a turning point, separating his old life from the present. Before the accident, he was high on life, a potent agent with a lot to look forward to. After the accident, he was depressed, helpless, and uncertain. The scope of his powerlessness was initially bounded to the present. He felt totally dependent, unable to take care of himself. During this period of pain and forced inactivity, Ray was unable or unwilling to draw out future implications too precisely or clearly. He could no longer become the person he anticipated becoming, nor live the course of life he anticipated living. Dislodged from a life story, Ray preferred indefiniteness for in uncertainty, there was still hope. What was becoming clear as a dreaded potential was a life of dependency.

There was no control over the paralysis. It controlled him, but within limitations, Ray could set goals. He set goals to eat on his own without tubes, to be able to sit up and see outside, to be able to grab drinks from the stand, to build up his arms while enduring the pain in his hips from lying so much, and to be home in his own bed by his sixteenth birthday. The goals allowed him to gain some sense of control, to preserve his mental well-being, and to feel more active. It was a great feeling to beat the odds and as goals were reached, new and higher goals were formed.

By day, Ray projected toughness and optimism. Partially, it was a front, but never completely so. It was very important to maintain toughness and positivity, particularly as he was allowed to sit up and become more physically active. However, by night, he sometimes gave in to despair and cried. When his parents visited, he expressed his anger, bitterness, and frustration. Yet when his coach visited, he told him that he would return after Christmas. He just needed a little time to get back on his feet. Ray was working toward a more stable attitude, but it was difficult to achieve. Perhaps inadvertently, a physiotherapist cultivated a false hope that Ray might walk without crutches and braces, yet his legs never showed movement, no matter how much he willed them to. There was nothing certain in his situation, no solid ground for firm expectation, and the prospect of being a paraplegic for life was hard to accept all at once.

While Ray wavered emotionally, he remained steady in striving to achieve reachable goals. Being able to use braces to stand, walking with a walker, using the wheelchair, self-care, transferring from wheelchair to bed, there was a lot to learn. He had to build up his upper body, develop coordination, and learn how things were done. Whether he felt upbeat or down, he maintained a discipline of striving toward goals.

Ray was scheduled to move to a rehabilitation center, but he would have to wait two months. Instead of waiting, he wanted to go home. A physician tried to change his mind. "If you were my son, I would recommend to you that you stay in the hospital another month and a half where they can help you with basic care and at least some rehabilitation." This fatherly advice cut through Ray's resistance and he stayed. Looking back, Ray regards this decision as pivotal. Going home without total rehabilitation would have been over-whelming, leading to defeat, depression, and dependence. It would have been too much to manage while retaining a spir-ited effort to rehabilitate himself. At least in retrospect, readi-ness seemed crucial to maintain progress.

Ray was moved to a geriatric ward to wait, but it was too depressing and he requested a private room. There was an older paraplegic on the ward who had been admitted for bed sores. He drank all the time, a broken man who seemed to make it through life by staying drunk. For Ray, this was the first model of a paraplegic that he had an opportunity to observe, and he was repulsed. "No way," he thought, "I'm not going to be like this guy." Ray kept an image of this man in the back of his mind as he practiced, a negative model of his future that he must strive to avoid at all costs.

Throughout his stay in the hospital, Ray was supported by good relations with student nurses. They were like big sis-ters and one became an enduring friend. Sometimes he flirted, but not seriously. Romance, he thought, was just not going to happen. He could dream, but that was all. Never-theless, as his leg muscles atrophied, became thin and ugly in his view, he covered them up. He did not want to face his dis-ability just yet, nor did he want others to see. It made him feel more shy than usual, embarrassed.

Toward the end as he was getting ready to move to the rehabilitation center, Ray became upset. He was nervous. The hospital routine had become comfortable and familiar. It was no longer very challenging, but it was known territory. He knew what to expect and had some degree of control. At the rehabilitation center, he was not sure what to expect. He felt quite vulnerable again, not at all confident.

The rehabilitation center was housed in an old barracks. It was musty smelling, depressing, and generally felt like a dungeon. From 8 A.M. to 4 P.M. it offered excellent technical help, and Ray concentrated on tangible, physical goals that would allow him to get home. Whether it was self-care (work on bowel and bladder) or standing on braces, Ray tended to pursue everything to the limit. He felt a tremendous sense of accomplishment in physical progress, standing briefly on braces or moving a short distance with the walker. Sometimes he tried to visualize what life would be like, how he would deal with dependency and his fear of dependency. Occasionally, he glimpsed fears hovering on the border of awareness, but avoided dwelling on them. As yet, they were too overwhelming. Instead, he focused upon "attainable, real issues of disability."

From 4 P.M. to bedtime, the rehabilitation center was less than ideal. It was boring and potentially depressing. Ray was confronted with many different attitudes, none of which seemed appealing or provided guidance. There was no model to follow, no one with whom he could identify. The majority of other patients seemed depressed and passive. Some complained all the time. Others were just passing time, waiting for a disability check to pay off luxury items such as stereo sets. Many drank a lot or took drugs.

Ray avoided other patients. He was not ready to sit back and accept his disability as just a fixed condition. For Ray, it was a fact that his legs were paralyzed and might never improve. However, his situation was not fixed; it had borders or frontiers that he could explore and push toward, if he were not dragged down by pessimism. What he could and could not do in the future was partially an open question that depended significantly upon his own efforts. Rather than socialize with other patients or just relax for lengthy periods of time each day, Ray felt challenged to work independently toward his goals, particularly practicing with braces.

Largely alone, Ray became lonely. There were few visitors. Sometimes as the emptiness built up, he made long distance calls just to make meaningful contact with someone. Even if it was after curfew, he would insist upon making a call. When institutional rules conflicted with his own sense of priority, Ray had no doubt which was to prevail.

His ventures into open environments were both exciting and sobering. In a public restaurant, he embarrassed himself by falling out a door into a garbage can. His brief visit home for Christmas was not a good experience. He was not yet proficient in brace walking and other skills, which left him much more dependent than he could accept. However, setbacks were simply the price of testing the frontiers of his disability. There is a fine line between shaping one's life and being shaped by conditions beyond one's control. This line changes over time with increased skill and maturity, yet would never be known without testing the limits of one's capacity. The rewards of testing are increased freedom, more control, and the utter exhilaration of striving against obstacles and occasionally winning. Ventures in open environments were confrontations with the real world through which he could gauge his progress and appreciate the significance of his practice.

After three months at the rehabilitation center, Ray was ready to go home. Administration was resistant because they expected he would need six months. To get out, he had to have his lawyer talk with them. Throughout his stay in the hospital and rehabilitation center, Ray had tried to interact with people who could help, support, and guide him toward a normal life. He depended on them largely for technical help. However, he was never compliant. He was selective, as capable of resisting influence as accepting it. He refused some recommended forms of therapy and ignored discouraging advice about braces, among other things. Each refusal involved a battle with administration. Perhaps because Ray had a clear view of what he wanted, he took partial responsibility for what was to happen in his rehabilitation. While administration was apparently used to passive obedience, Ray treated everything as a matter for negotiation. He judged orders, rules, requests, and activities in relation to his goals, fighting to maintain control of the various influences from others on his life. While these battles were prominent in his stay, they were secondary to the pursuit of goals. Striving, a spirited effort to reach goals was the dominant theme of his rehabilitation.

This period of preparation was dominated by an expanding series of agentic experiences. Through pursuing goals that were real and attainable, Ray achieved some mastery of his situation, practiced self-determination, and set the stage for tryouts in open environments. Like an athlete, he practiced and gauged progress. For Ray, the personal significance of progress, what stamped all efforts with a similar meaning, was that it boded well for living independently and reestablishing normality in his life. Very early, Ray construed his situation in a way that endowed practice with tremendous significance. However, as he struggled toward goals, practice was never just a means. Rather, it became something like an internal competition that was intrinsically motivated, an end in itself. Ray could lose himself in practice and experience something like the joy of athletic competition.

Nearly from the beginning, practice was an exploration. There were false hopes (e.g., that he would walk again) and real hopes (e.g., standing with braces), but he would never discover what was possible or impossible except by trying. Strikingly similar to Maddi's (1988) discussion of facticity and possibility, Ray's attitude came to be that one must swing "between what has to be and what might be to find the most." Progress is not just a matter of improved skill, for instance, but also an exploration and expansion of what might be, calling for a more complex construction of oneself and situations.

Pursuing goals takes place within a context that can support or hinder goal selection and striving. If Ray had been placed in an open environment (e.g., home) too soon, he would have been confronted with goals beyond his current capability and issues (e.g., dependence) that he was not yet ready to face constructively. The structure and routine of medical institutions provided a shelter in which he could pursue appropriate and attainable goals. Institutions also include rigidity in rules and cultivate rather confining attitudes, at least among some of the professionals. A significant part of Ray's progress seemed to depend upon self-determined selectivity, a willingness to accept advice and help along with a willingness to refuse them. As best he could, he exercised his own judgment on the influences around him, which required him at times to stand his ground against nurses, physicians, and administrators.

Of potential importance, Ray did not have positive models to follow, but he did have negative models to avoid at all costs. He steered away from one vision (a broken alcoholic), but what he was steering toward was general and ill-defined (e.g., normality, independence). At least, striving to avoid the negative supported his focus upon immediate goals. Possibly, a positive model would have prematurely expanded his focus to a course of life. While Ray tried to visualize his future life, he also could draw back when it began to seem overwhelming, and return to "attainable, real issues of disability." Upon these issues, he could act. Upon larger issues, he was rendered inactive and threatened.

Emotionally, Ray was in turmoil, wavering from the tough, upbeat posture of a recovering person to the vulnerable, lonely posture of one who had lost nearly everything. He had no stable position or orientation, but was in between, coming to terms with traumatic injury, and both postures reflected his situation. He had indeed lost his old life, and that loss perhaps had to be grieved, but if he clung to it, he would interfere with the development of a new life. However, the fragments of a new life were scarcely evident; they would elaborate and crystallize as he pursued goals. Yet at the same time, there was so little foundation that Ray felt like he was putting on a front, but a front that eventually became real. Following the logic of a rite of passage, this wavering facilitates detachment from the old and attachment to the new.

Perhaps of considerable importance here is what might be termed personal support. Among some nurses, he made friends and even flirted. They made him feel like a person and helped sustain him through the difficult periods. And at times, he actively sought this kind of support, calling people in his hometown. While this kind of support was clearly important to Ray, it is not capable of being assigned a clear and definite function. Rather, the caring that seems central in personal relationships enlivens an indefinite number of functions such as facilitating understanding, self-esteem, and stability.

In summary, this phase of Ray's rehabilitation can be aptly summarized as preparation or positioning. He has been thrown out of a livable position and is attempting to regain one, wavering between what was lost and what might be. Positioning ranges from selecting and shaping settings to developing physical skills, and larger, a tentative orientation to life as a paraplegic.

In going home, Ray had insisted upon a car and a room in the basement with his own washroom, two important aids toward independence. After a crash course in driving, his father picked him up. Once again, Ray was upset and nervous about leaving a secure environment for the unknown, but it had to be done. He drove home with his father. He drove very slowly and once spun off the road into a snow bank where they were stuck for a few hours. When they were finally helped out, Ray drove the rest of the way home, with forceful encouragement from his father.

Ray was apprehensive about returning to school and being with old friends. He had been a star athlete; now he was a cripple. Worried about his status, he wanted to appear as normal as possible. Rejecting the wheelchair as a symbol of disability, he used braces. It seemed important to greet others standing up. At the time, braces seemed as close to normality as he could get and he regarded a wheelchair with scorn.

While Ray yearned for normality, life was anything but normal. The house seemed specially designed to obstruct a paraplegic and the school presented its own difficulties. For Ray, this period of adjusting to open environments was extremely frustrating. Everything was such a challenge, and because of the cold weather and ice, even the spaces he should have been able to negotiate were treacherous. On his first day at school, he had fallen in the snow before he had even reached the door. Self-conscious, these public accidents were certainly embarrassing, but in a way, they were acceptable, as familiar as sport. The challenge was a physical one, and Ray knew that through practice, he would improve. He would have to endure the frustration and continue the discipline of practice.

More difficult, however, were other problems. Ray thought that he would be too unattractive for dating. Who would want to go out with him? And he thought that he would not have much of a social life. Who would want to be a friend of a paraplegic? How could he participate in normal activities of friends such as dancing or swimming? To these problems, he had no answers, nothing he could practice. He would just have to wait and see.

The worst part of the day at school was gym. He both longed to be there and hated it. So few months before, he had virtually lived for sport. He had been a part of the gym activities. Now, he could not take part and he felt devastated. In gym, all the sparkle of his old life confronted the bleakness of his current situation.

This conflict between old aspirations and present realities began to change when his coach asked him to be an assistant coach for the team. It took awhile to feel comfortable and then he began to enjoy coaching. It was a new role in sport, one he had not envisioned before, but it felt good. It offered its own satisfactions and allowed him to participate in a different way, like a door opening when they had all seemed to be locked shut.

Other opportunities arose. After only moments, his friends turned out to still be friends and they continued to do things together. A stranger, S, got him involved in wheelchair sport. For the first time, Ray was exposed to disabled persons with whom he could identify, who could serve as role models. A girl in class began smiling at him and finally she asked Ray out. They went out for about three months. Ray became interested in another girl, P, and ended up going steady with her for three years.

Within a few months, Ray was busy with several spheres of life. While he trained for competitions in wheelchair sport, he coached individuals and teams. He dated, hung out with friends, and concentrated on school work. He even began to dance with his wheelchair. Life expanded rapidly and Ray began to consider what he could bring back. What would he have to adapt to? He took advantage of what he could, and as he did, questions began to arise. Do I like myself? Do I like my life?

Ray had to readjust his thinking. The barriers to involvement in something like a full life were not so much external as internal. What held him back was himself. While he was very vocal and firm about speaking up for things he believed in, he did not yet believe in himself. Ray was insecure, did not believe he was worthwhile, lacked confidence as a human being, and had a poor body image. Ray tended to gauge himself by physical attributes, overemphasizing his weaknesses and failing to recognize his strengths.

Little things would set him off, put him in a sour mood that could last a short time or a few days. Being helped to a cabin might trigger an exaggerated view of his dependence. If someone looked at P, Ray might feel deflated by comparison. Later, he regretted his reactions. It did not make sense to feel such pain. Ray began to question his reactions, to relive these scenarios and try to understand them.

P helped Ray throughout this turmoil of adjustment. Initially, Ray had difficulty participating in some activities such as swimming and it took a long time to swim without sweatpants covering his legs. Sitting on the sideline, he questioned his fears and yearned. As he grew in trust and assurance, he learned to accept help in order to do what he wanted to do. Still later, he learned to value activities in themselves without spoiling them by reference to the past and how it used to be. None of the activities he loved could be the same, he recognized, but they still have value.

Through his relationship with P, Ray gained confidence and a sense of fulfillment. He felt complete, not as if he were always lacking. The relationship shifted his rather narrow emphasis upon the physical to other qualities. Ray learned that he was fun to be with and sensitive, that he had many good qualities. Perhaps of even more importance, he learned that he could have a meaningful relationship with a woman. Later, Ray came to a view a relationship as a mirror that reflects oneself. One's qualities, problems, strengths, and weaknesses are shown right back.

Ray was also successful in other areas of life. In wheelchair sport, he won some competitions and became more deeply involved in the possibilities of athletic participation. His coaching was rewarded when one of the athletes he personally helped, a friend, was selected for an exclusive team.

Ray felt like he was part of this person's success. After graduation, he worked for a year at two different jobs and took college preparatory courses. Over a period of about two and a half years, from when he returned home to a year after graduation, Ray recovered his life. He had found meaningful activities in which he could participate, meaningful relationships, and good qualities in himself. Gradually, gains had been consolidated amid the setbacks and difficulties of striving. Even when he scalded his foot and reexperienced all the horrors of dependency, he was still able to appreciate what had been accomplished, how far he had come. He was now ready to venture further and entered a university away from home.

Ray experienced university as a wonderful expansion and development. There were so many opportunities and different people. On the wheelchair basketball team, he got to know other disabled persons and how they dealt with their lives, the different philosophies of people, many of whom were worthy models. In classes, he had to overcome his shyness and give talks. He was finally accepted into the School of Physical Education, which was like a dream come true. Over the summer, he continued in wheelchair sport.

Ray had been living with a friend from his hometown. He now asked that friend to move out. Ray wanted to be by himself, to try living independently. He was ready, and in a way, had outgrown the past. His friend was part of the old world of his hometown and might cramp the way he now wanted to shape his life.

During this period, Ray sought to reestablish his life. He entered situations in which opportunities were available or extended to him. Taking advantage of opportunities was not something he practiced for, but something he readied himself for. A coach asked him to be an assistant. A stranger drew him into wheelchair sport. A girl asked him for a date. Friends included him in outings. By acting on these opportunities, life expanded rapidly with roles, relationships, and activities.

As his life began to fill up, with one thing leading to another, experiences stimulated more and more reflection. He acted and reflected. He refrained from acting (e.g., not going swimming with others) and reflected. A vigorous cycle of participation and spectatorship was established, allowing Ray to enact and then to imaginatively revise, extend, or refine various scenarios for living. For example, one could accept necessary help and make the most of a situation or one could be offended by help and withdraw into a morose contemplation of one's fallen state. Two plots, each of which had far-reaching implications for a larger pattern of life. Greatly assisting Ray in this cycle were personal relationships. Others not only supported his participation in activities, but also stimulated more constructive reflection that guided him toward the elaboration of more agentic plot lines.

Elaboration of an agentic plot took two general directions. First, Ray recognized that the major barrier to participation in activities was his own attitude. He felt insecure, inferior, and vulnerable, and tended to enact this kind of story while yearning for another, more positive one. Major developments toward a positive involvement include the following. He learned to accept help when needed. He valued activities in themselves without spoiling them by a comparison to the past. He shifted self-evaluation from physical attributes to personal qualities such as sensitivity. He accepted the more positive view of himself that was reflected back in relationships. He was successful in what he undertook. In this way, he came to experience a completeness in roles, activities, and relationships, replacing the sense of lack that pervaded his experiences previously.

Second, as his activities expanded, Ray came to evaluate the shape his life was taking and to choose future directions and courses of action. Released, in a sense, from the demands of the present, urgent problems and lacks, he evaluated himself and his life more broadly. To further expand meant, in part, giving up or leaving behind relationships and securities, yet through refusing to cling, Ray gained more opportunities, worthy models, deeper involvement in sport, and a sense of independence.

In general, this period of rapid expansion was concerned with positing or actualizing a vision of the good life. Certainly, there was no detailed script that he merely had to live, but rather an outline that had to be revised and elaborated as he moved along. In a way, what Ray recovered was authorial control over his life story, moving from one who was shaped by disability to one who could shape life in a fulfilling way.

Living independently, Ray was high on life. He was getting to do what it seemed he had always wanted to do and was confident in how he wanted to shape his life further. His legs were not like an anchor holding him down. He could talk about his disability and no longer felt bad about it. All the good things in his life crystallized with perfect clarity, and he did not ruin these things by comparison with what used to be or by unrealistic values. It had taken a redefinition of life, acceptance of what he could not control and disciplined striving for what he could attain, but his life finally emerged with incredible force as something that was precious. Ray had always felt that life was valuable, and believes that this sense supported his efforts from the beginning, but now it was as if a potential had become actual and enduring.

One day, Ray tried to get friends to go with him on a fishing trip. No one wanted to go. Finally, Ray caught himself depending on others and wondered why he could not go by himself. He packed up and drove over an hour to a fishing spot he had known in youth. Where he stopped, there was a fence between him and the river. "Why should I let this deter me," he thought. He struggled over the fence with his wheelchair and gear. To get to the river, he had to go up hill, through a ditch, over a barbed wire fence, through a meadow, and down a hill. It was a good feeling being able to do it as he had before. As he sat beside the river and fished, he appreciated his accomplishment. It was a good day.

The fishing was not very good and Ray decided to try his luck on another plateau lower down. He went too fast and tipped over the embankment into the river. Quickly reaching, he caught a hold on the side and then grabbed his wheelchair before it sunk. Through the mud and vegetation on the embankment, Ray pulled himself and his wheelchair up. When he reached the top and settled back into the wheelchair, he did so not just with relief, but with an exhilarating sense of independence and accomplishment. There was something deeply symbolic about the fishing trip and it remains as the culmination of his struggle to regain potency as the agent or main character of his own life story.

Clearly, Ray reached a sense of completion, ending the story of his rehabilitation and beginning a new story. Of particular interest, however, is the culminating event. In part, this event serves as a marker that divides life into before and after. It signals a return to life as he wished it, very similar to incorporation into a new status that ends a rite of passage. Yet the story of this event means more still. It remains in Ray's memory as an instructive story to guide the conduct of his life, a concrete plot for a larger plot of living. And the structure of the plot is a compressed expression of the story of his recovery as a whole, one that offers continuity with life before the accident.

Before the accident, Ray had been headstrong, eager for challenges and able to strive alone. Life was good, just as it was in overcoming barriers to go fishing. After the accident, desperate action was required just to survive, but also by determined action, he could pull himself up to a higher place that was also exhilarating and filled with a sense not only of accomplishment, but of independence. It was still a good day and still a good life.

Tom's Narrative

At the time of the interviews, Tom was thirty-eight years old and had recently married. The second eldest of five children, Tom grew up in a small town where his life was devoted to sports. At age seventeen, he suffered spinal cord injury in a diving accident. Both arms and legs were paralyzed, and he was unable to breath without the use of a ventilator. At the present time, Tom is a rehabilitation counselor while enrolled in a clinical counseling training program. He is very active sitting on committees, giving workshops and presentations, helping to organize conferences, and speaking on behalf of many organizations.

Tom accidentally dove into a lake where the water was only three feet deep. After a friend pulled him out of the water and onto the beach, Tom thought he had had the wind knocked out of him which was a familiar feeling as an athlete. He felt desperate when it did not pass. He was struggling for all he was worth to breathe. It felt like coming up from the bottom of a pool for air and having somebody push you back down again. When his friend lifted him up, at his request, and he saw his foot go off to the side, he knew he had no control over his body. Whatever was wrong was serious, perhaps a broken back. After an ambulance transported him to a hospital, and having passed out more than once, Tom experienced a beautiful sensation, a gust of air. They had performed a tracheotomy on him and he was finally able to breathe. From that point on, it was the beginning of a new life that was downhill for a long time.

The first thoughts Tom had when he became aware of the severity of his injury were very depressing ones. "I'll never be married. I'll never be able to contribute. I have no purpose or value. I am a total leech." Eventually, one of the few things Tom looked forward to were points of progress in his physical development. However, these points were usually not as exciting as he anticipated them to be. For instance, after being in traction for five or six months to keep his neck straight, Tom could not wait to get the tongs off his head so he could sit up and look around. He did not anticipate how weak his neck would be. The nurse would wind up the head of his bed one crank and he would feel like passing out. He would ask the nurse to put him back down, but she would not, insisting that it was good for him. Tom was frustrated and angry because he felt the nurse was unable to understand the pain he was in and was refusing to respond to his wishes. It was probably one of the first times that Tom knew that other people were in control of his life. It felt like they were making all the decisions, and it seemed like he had no input into what was being done to his own body.

After seeing himself in a mirror for the first time, five months after the accident, Tom was devastated and wanted to go back to bed immediately because he looked so disabled. He wanted to stay in bed with the sheet up to his neck so that he could just look like he was sick in bed; his disability would be hidden. For months, Tom resisted getting out of bed because he was so ashamed of the body that had been a point of pride before the accident. Before his injury, Tom related to himself as a physical specimen that could score x number of goals a year. His status as a hockey player afforded him a kind of small-town idol worship. His value was as a hockey player and now that those physical attributes were gone, his value seemed gone.

During the first year of depression and devastation, there were two interrelated themes of experience. First, Tom was overwhelmed by the immensity of what he had lost. He would never marry, contribute to anything, and so on. In short, he lost a life, and underwent a dying to himself (the loss of purpose, of value, of status, of promise). Second, he was confronted with what he had become. Using his past life and frame of meaning as a comparison, he had become a repulsive, useless, helpless leech. His accident emplotted him in a story in which he would leech from others until he died. That was his present and future, and it was vividly portrayed by his physical appearance. Tom was so ashamed of what he had become that he wanted to hide. As yet, small physical gains were not very exciting, and in any case, came not through his own decision and efforts, but through others deciding and acting on him.

Tom was totally ventilator-dependent. That is, an air pump was hooked into a trache (a fitting in his neck) which allowed him to breathe. He was told by doctors that he would never breathe on his own again. Tom was frightened to think of being totally dependent on a machine for each breath he took. A year after the injury, one doctor said to Tom, "I think you might be able to breathe a little bit on your own." The doctor took the ventilator off and there was some movement of air. Tom was excited and hopeful. He knew that his paralysis would never change. Being paralyzed was one thing, but being ventilator-dependent was quite another. If he could somehow overcome his dependence on the ventilator it would feel like he had lost fifty percent of his dependence. He also thought that if he could breathe on his own for even five minutes, he would be able to provide himself with emergency backup in case of a machine breakdown. Breathing for five minutes on his own became his goal.

At first, it was the toughest thing in the world to go for two minutes of breathing on his own. He used to be able to hold his breath for that long. Now it felt like running a marathon without ever having trained for it. At the same time, it felt good because it provided him with at least some indication of physical development. Physical ability was the only frame of reference Tom had known. Tom's enthusiasm, however, was not shared by all his doctors. They felt that his practice would be futile and dangerous for his heart. It was also inconvenient for them because it meant that a staff member had to be present during practice times for safety reasons. This discouragement and opposition did not stop Tom. Instead, he solicited the help of his sister. She would take the ventilator off, monitor him as he practiced, and just before he passed out, put it back on. He trusted his sister with his life. Ironically, it was Tom's sister who became the target for much of his anger and frustration. He criticized and belittled her relentlessly.

Breathing without the ventilator was difficult and exhausting work. It felt good though to push himself and to discipline himself as he had done in sports. It gave him something to strive for. Having a goal represented having some control over his life. He could measure and monitor his day-to-day progress and project ahead to future improvement.

Two months later, after attaining his goal of five minutes, he set himself a new challenge of ten minutes. He wanted to achieve this goal as a Christmas gift to his parents. When Christmas came, however, he had a negative reaction to a drug he had been given and almost died. He was disappointed at not having met the time line and at not being able to give this gift to his parents. After he recovered, he continued practicing despite the setback. At this point, the goal was to increase the time off the ventilator, but there was no specific time line to strive for, which made it harder. He was also uncertain as to whether or not he could even increase his time. The lack of a specific goal coupled with the uncertainty frequently led Tom to become lazy about his practice. For instance, despite the fact that damage to the heart was a legitimate concern, Tom often used it as an excuse to avoid practice. Although his practice was not steady and regular, he eventually worked himself up to half an hour after a year. With half an hour under his belt, he imagined going a little longer and perhaps being able to get away from the hospital.

At one point, Tom's father responded to his efforts by saying, "Son, only you know how really tough it is. Don't let other people influence your goals, don't push yourself to meet others' expectations." Tom knew that his father thought he might have been overdoing it and it might be too hard for him. For Tom, it was a moment of clarity, but not in the way his father had intended it to be. To Tom, part of being institutionalized had involved giving up his control. Having others do everything for him became a way of life. He had come to expect it. Suddenly in that moment, Tom realized that it was indeed totally up to him to breathe on his own for longer periods of time. No one else could do it for him. Despite his father's intent to ease his struggle, it had just the opposite effect; it spurred him on.

After about two years, Tom was able to go for two and a half hours on his own without the use of a ventilator. A friend with whom Tom felt comfortable invited him to go on a two-hour car trip to a nearby town. This was the first time that there would not be a ventilator available to Tom for backup purposes. He knew he could do it, but he was not sure if he could do it with any composure. He was afraid to put F in an uncomfortable position and he did not want to put himself in the position of having to depend on F. As the trip took longer than anticipated, the last half hour was a real struggle, but he made it. Tom felt a new sense of independence and freedom having made the trip. It left him wondering what he could accomplish next.

The doctor who had told Tom that he would never breathe on his own again was amazed at hearing of Tom's breathing achievements. Tom felt satisfied to have proven him wrong. For the next seven years, Tom continued his arduous practice. At the present time, Tom can breathe on his own all day and uses a ventilator at night while he is sleeping. Each breath remains a conscious effort.

To Tom, the hospital felt like a prison with endless restrictions and regulations, and a total lack of privacy. He felt helpless there. Tom rebelled against the system, and when the other patients would remind him that if he did not cooperate he would lose his "privileges," Tom was amused because he did not feel he had any to lose. Hospital staff disciplined Tom's non-compliant behavior (such as drinking or being late) with lectures or by taking his wheelchair and clothes away. On one occasion, the supervisor threatened to ship him off to another facility 2,000 miles away. She said, "You're a bad influence on the whole ward! You're causing a lot of disturbances." It was at this moment that Tom was struck by the influence he had on the system. He was having an impact, regardless of whether it was positive or negative, it was an effect. It helped him to feel some sense of potency. Tom replied to the supervisor's threat by saying, "Great, go ahead. I have friends there." His sarcastic retort was to show her that she did not have as much power over him as she thought. He did not care what she said and called her bluff. Once again, someone had made a comment to Tom and the effect had been the opposite of what was intended.

In addition to being told that he would never breathe on his own again, Tom was told that he would never leave the hospital. He desperately wanted to go home for a visit; it was safe there. He was told that no one outside the hospital was capable of looking after him. To Tom, it was apparent that this was not the case. He had been out of the hospital for periods of time, so it did not make sense that he could not go for several days at a time. Despite their intent to help, the attitudes of people in authority created endless roadblocks and obstacles which only served to restrict and to limit Tom. Tom soon learned that the people in authority did not know everything, let alone what was best for him.

After two years of recovery and against the advice of hospital staff, Tom began visits home despite his fear about leaving the security of the hospital and traveling 750 miles by air. Tom was deeply affected by his father's response to the doctor's stern warning, "If you take him home, you'll kill him." "Well," his father said, "Then we'll bring him back dead." People in charge at the hospital had an attitude of, "You can't do that!" Tom's family, and in time Tom, had an attitude of "Why not?"

Tom did survive his visits home and over time began to increase the length of his stay. There was a ceiling on how long the hospital would hold the bed in his absence. Tom disregarded these rules which created many power struggles with hospital staff. Instead of making him conform, these incidents energized Tom. Through the support of his family, which Tom considers vital to his rehabilitation and transformation, Tom felt safe enough to risk challenging the hospital system rather than to passively accept their definition of how he was to live his life. Tom's family responded to what he wanted, not in a senseless way, but in a way that respected his decisions about his own body and the direction he wanted to go. Through supporting his decisions, they empowered him. Through risking with him, they helped him to begin to see an alternative way of living beyond the hospital walls.

Even though the hospital felt like a prison to Tom, it also offered security; it was a safe haven from the real world. Tom would never leave the hospital except with a family member. Going out with other people meant facing his dependence and feeling vulnerable. It meant asking others for help; to wipe his nose, to feed him, to take care of the basics. At least in the hospital someone was paid to do it. For instance, if he was with someone and there was something in his eye, he would tolerate the discomfort to avoid asking for help. The ultimate in humiliation was asking someone to empty his urinary leg bag.

For Tom, not being able to manage bodily functions on his own was like being an infant again. Unlike an infant, however, as an adult this inability was embarrassing. To avoid embarrassing situations it was best to stay in the hospital. At least in the hospital Tom could function and not look like an incompetent. To be away from the hospital and the people that understood his needs was a real risk which made Tom feel vulnerable. In order to deal with his feelings of vulnerability and dependence, Tom always tried to present an attitude to having no needs related to his disability. He was determined right from the beginning to never put anyone in the position of having to do anything that they were uncomfortable with. Consequently, Tom chose to stay in the hospital as much as possible as a means of self-protection.

One of the first times Tom went out of the hospital with friends rather than with family was very difficult. A woman friend who had known Tom hrough hockey invited him to a birthday celebration. Tom grew more apprehensive and anxious as the date of the party approached. Despite wanting to go to the party, it meant that this woman friend would see how physically powerless he was in contrast to his previous physical powerfulness. He knew he should go, but he did not want to feel vulnerable. In female company, Tom was even more aware of his feelings of incompetence. His fear was making people uncomfortable if he needed to ask for help. To ease his anxiety and to take the edge off, Tom invited another male friend to accompany him. Tom probably would not have gone if his friend had been unable to go with him.

In this period of preparation, setting a goal and pursuing it has salvational significance. The goal constitutes, if not a way out, a mode of improvement, a movement from passive dependence toward more active independence. Success is marked by feelings of independence, control, and freedom. Pursuing a goal is strengthened by success, specificity, confidence that it is within one's capability, and ownership, a recognition that attaining a goal depends upon one's own efforts and is one's chosen struggle. In Tom's account, these features are all noted, sometimes as striking moments of illumination.

Pursuing a goal organizes life. Other people become supportive or hindering, and this support or hindrance can make a striking difference. Support from Tom's family was crucial for his progress. For example, the medical personnel would not help him practice breathing; he had to get the help of his sister. The setting in which one pursues a goal has supports and hindrances. In one sense, it is a shelter that offers security and routine, a refuge from issues that are too overwhelming at the time. In another sense, it is like a prison with regulations and restrictions and expectations of compliance that create obstacles. It is an oddity of the situation that a person might gain a sense of potency by defying or influencing the setting and its system of control, the very one that shelters the struggle. Pursuing a goal, in any case, is not done in isolation, but seems to require a person to confront and overcome active interference and lack of support from other people and the setting.

Eventually, as improvement in pursuing a goal expands to other settings, or supports other possibilities, such as attending a birthday celebration, a person is confronted with supports and hindrances from oneself, one's own beliefs and attitudes. Particularly since Tom was in such a vulnerable state, feeling like a useless, worthless, and repulsive leech, internal barriers seem inevitable. While the fuller struggle against internal barriers is apt to be prominent later when one attempts to actualize aspects of a good life, these barriers appear to be engaged early on during preparation.

Most often, friends would come to visit Tom in the hospital. Tom soon discovered that under those smiling, supportive faces, and able bodies, was a lot of pain. Through talking with them, he began to understand that he was fulfilling some of their needs. Being able to give to others helped him to begin to feel a sense of worth. It was a potent feeling to give where he never thought he could give again. Eventually, things snowballed and there were great demands on Tom's time and he had to begin scheduling it. He had never imagined this in his wildest dreams. He had wondered how he was going to occupy even a few minutes in his life let alone twelve to fourteen hours of each day. It became apparent to Tom that he could contribute, in what he felt was a significant way, to other people's lives.

Five years after the injury, Tom began to receive a number of requests from doctors and nurses to talk to incoming patients with similar injuries. He discovered that he was able to help ease their pain and exert a positive effect by helping them to mature in their injury. He helped them to see that there really was life after quadriplegia. Tom again felt like he was contributing, giving rather than just receiving. It was very fulfilling and enhanced his growing sense of self-worth. Before long, Tom was being asked to travel farther and farther afield in order to provide counseling to people with physical disabilities.

The accident forced Tom to confront some very fundamental questions. Where is my value? Who am I now? What is my purpose? Through becoming a Christian, answers to these questions became clearer. After the accident Tom had seen himself as a mere shadow of his former self because he had no physical ability. He realized now that his value did not only lie in his physical attributes. He was the same person, just with a different set of limitations and a different set of open horizons. He chose to focus on what he could do, not what he could not do. Christianity gave him an understanding of his existence just as he was rather than as he had been; a framework within which to make sense out of his disability. It gave him direction and helped him to define his purpose. It provided important insight into the pain and suffering, and the peace and joy that existed within him and within the world.

Around this time, Tom traveled to Asia and Europe with members of his family. Although he was apprehensive about traveling to such faraway countries, he went ahead anyway. Tom had many trying but exciting experiences which filled him with a sense of being able to do anything he wanted to do with the right attitude and the right approach. The right attitude was that nothing is impossible and anything is possible. The right approach was to not let yourself or anyone around you become overwhelmed.

Tom was able to apply these learnings to many situations. For instance, one time Tom needed to get home and there was no one available to accompany him. He knew the airlines would not allow him to travel alone. It was one of those opportunities where he had to take control because he knew best what he was capable of. He got a friend to put him on the airplane and arranged for someone to meet him at the other end. When the flight attendant asked him who was riding with him, Tom replied in a rather general way that his escort was behind him. There really were eighty other people on the plane sitting behind him, so Tom did not really feel like he was lying. With that obstacle out of the way, Tom knew he was going to have to deal with three stops on the flight. Each stop meant that he would fall forward in his seat because of the momentum. Each time the airplane landed, a new person would board. In flight, Tom would initiate some casual conversation until the comfort level increased a bit. Then as they approached landing Tom would say in a very casual, calm, matter of fact voice, "Oh, just when we land here, if you wouldn't mind putting your arm across my chest so I don't lean forward."

The main thing for Tom was to project to others that he was confident and in control in order to disarm their anxiety and to get them to work with him, not against him. The minute he showed that he was not in control, people would panic and try to take control (which was not usually the best thing for Tom). Tom also learned that it was up to him as to how other people saw him. He knew that he was the "unknown" with the wheelchair, the disability, the trache, and the ventilator. He could do nothing and allow people to feel threatened or he could reach out and make people feel comfortable. Being able to affect his relationships with other people gave him a sense of control.

In 1979, Tom and a friend from the hospital got together and approached an organization that dealt with disability issues to discuss the possibility of moving out of the hospital into an independent living setting within the community. Tom wondered why the institution had to be his only option for a home. The idea was well received, and one particular individual became very active in developing the project. Together, they launched an investigation of the various issues involved in such an undertaking (e.g., cost, staffing, safety). They discovered that the cost to the government would be fifty percent less than for them to stay in the hospital. For Tom, and others involved in the project, the main task ended up being one of finding ways to circumvent the fears of the hospital administration and to pacify government officials of potential law suits should anything happen to any of them. These attitudes were the biggest barriers Tom and the others had to face, not the project itself or their disabilities.

Over the next five years there were many ups and downs, triumphs and defeats. Tom's main focus throughout was on the goal which was to escape from the dependency of the hospital. He would do whatever it took to get the job done. In 1984, sixteen years after his injury, Tom and five other men with quadriplegia moved out of the hospital into their new home. Nothing like this had ever been done before so the project attracted a lot of international attention. People from around the world came to visit because there was an interest in implementing the same kind of project in other countries such as Scotland, Australia, and New Zealand. A documentary was also made.

Breathing without a ventilator offered freedom from total dependence, but what he would then be free to do was unclear. He wanted to be able to contribute, to do something meaningful, but what? The beginning of an answer arose unexpectedly in simply listening to and trying to help friends. Acting on further opportunities provided by doctors and nurses, Tom expanded his counseling activities. As his talent was recognized and he experienced satisfaction in helping others, counseling crystallized as a way he could contribute. It required a broader understanding of disability issues which, among other things, culminated in a plan to establish an independent setting for quadriplegics. The success of this project and Tom's growing reputation as a counselor led to other opportunities such as sitting on boards, speaking, and doing workshops. One thing led to another, eventually creating a sphere of related activities, a richness that he could not have conceived in the beginning efforts.

As his activities expanded, Tom had to overcome barriers within himself. Christianity offered a basis for a broader evaluation of himself, one that went beyond physical attributes to highlight a quite different set of virtues. Further, it provided insight into his condition and that of others, emphasized what he could do rather than what he could not do, and clarified his purpose in counseling. Tom became oriented toward possibility, taking care that he was never overwhelmed. This orientation required a more proactive stance toward others and situations, and detailed, realistic appraisal. It also required him to act in spite of fear and doubt, involving to some extent the development of a front that allowed him to appear much more confident and in control than he really was.

To Tom, independent living represented taking back his life. It provided the basics such as privacy, the freedom to come and go as he pleased, and responsibilities such as hiring and firing staff. Living in the community enabled Tom to better see where he could contribute. He got more involved in various ways such as doing workshops, presentations, speeches, and lectures. He began a clinical counseling training program. Tom knew that while it might not have been apparent to others, the quality of life and living had vastly improved for him.

Two years after moving out of the hospital, Tom received a call from a local political representative inviting him to sit on the board of directors for a committee on disability issues. Up to this point, Tom had not been directly involved in disability issues in any larger political sense. He felt completely inadequate for the job and was convinced that he would not have much to contribute. He agreed to participate despite these feelings. Over time, Tom gained an understanding of the issues and the process involved in getting things done. Later, he was asked to chair the committee. Again, despite his feeling that others were more qualified for the job, he accepted. The job required making a lot of major decisions. Tom was able to see that he could have a profound influence on a larger scale not just one on one. He could make a difference and have an impact. The whole thing was frightening and intimidating, but it was also highly meaningful. It provided Tom with an opportunity to discover what other skills he had aside from his counseling abilities.

Tom was now living independently. He was actively contributing in a variety of ways. He had many friends. He had not yet tackled anything beyond friendship; that was still too intimidating. Women had expressed a romantic interest in him, but Tom would quickly distance himself. He did not want to be that vulnerable. Surely once they saw him for who he was with all his limitations, they would reject him. He was no longer Tom the hockey player, he was Tom the quadriplegic. He was especially amazed that women who did not know him before the accident were attracted to him. When it happened repeatedly he could not dismiss it. It was very flattering.

Tom had refused several marriage proposals and in each case felt that he was doing the loving thing for the other person. Then Tom met W. They began a friendship in 1985 and when the subject of marriage eventually came up, it was dismissed immediately as it had been in the past. This time, however, W posed some questions to Tom that were to have a decisive influence on him. "What do you need to work on and what do you need to feel good about before you could marry?" Tom knew that it was because he still did not feel good about himself and did not think anyone else should be saddled with him for a lifetime in marriage. At this point, Tom made a decision. He was going to expose to W his real self, with all of his shortcomings and all of his limitations. He would become transparent and tear down the facade that was always in place. It would be a test. It was a difficult time for both Tom and W, but it did not change W's desire to marry him.

Tom was still not ready. There were more walls to tear down. Tom felt uncomfortable with not earning an income. How would he support himself and a wife? Tom had adopted an attitude of not needing anyone or not being dependent on anyone. He guarded against becoming attached and was doubtful about whether he could tear down that twenty-year-old wall. Intellectually, he knew that a healthy relationship involved both independence and dependence, but questioned whether he could show his needs and be dependent because it meant being vulnerable.

In time, Tom realized that it was simply not fair to another person not to show your need for them because you are not letting them see their real value. Tom knew how it felt not to be valued. By now, Tom developed a style of taking risks despite his fear. He felt able to risk for three reasons. One, he felt totally supported by his family. Two, his belief in God facilitated his sense of worth and purpose. Three, intellectually he believed that nothing would change and he would stay forever where he was in his fear if he did not risk. He did not like where he was, even though it was usually more comfortable, so he chose to face the fear instead. Frequently, Tom would discover that the vulnerability he so desperately feared was not as bad as he anticipated it to be. In 1989, Tom and W were married.

Courtship and marriage culminated Tom's transformation. As a story, it encapsulates major parts of the larger story of moving from passive taking to active giving. Further, it consolidates the plot of living that Tom now lives, a reasoned approach in which he acts in spite of fear and vulnerability, gaining from each venture a greater sense of purpose and worth. The option to retreat is always there, offering a security that is analogous to his first year of total dependency. One would be secure perhaps, but also feel useless. It is not really an option, yet it lingers on as a mirage of old emotions, fueling his determination to confront vulnerabilities in order to live more productively.

Pattern of Transformation

In the accounts of Ray and Tom, there appear to be four phases that follow one another like acts in a stage play. While these phases are clearly different, they overlap and interdepend, providing a natural progression from beginning to end. The beginning is dominated by entrapment in a sense of incompleteness. The middle involves two phases. First, one prepares or positions oneself for a return to active life. Second, one acts to recover a life. The end is pervaded by liberation into a sense of completion.

Incompleteness

The accident violently separates the old life from the present, forcing one into the role of a spectator on one's own deterioration (withering of muscles, distortion of appearance, etc.). A person becomes vividly aware of what one is not or is no longer. Awareness might be stalled by false hopes, refusing to dwell on implications, and perhaps even denial, but there are too many bleak reminders to do so comfortably, such as pain, immobility, and dependence. Gradually, awareness expands, drawing out two opposing plots. Before the accident, one was in control, competent, useful, and free. After one is controlled, helpless, useless, and confined, a "leech" or "total dependent." The positivity of one drama fuels the negativity of the other, and as a person dwells on the contrast, comes to elaborate the present primarily by what it lacks.

The gap between the old life and the new, what is and what ought to be, provides ground for the significant experiences of this period such as depression, helplessness, anger, fear, and the like. However, the constructive function of the gap is to provide inspiration for recovery. Living a nightmare, while memory of a better life is yet fresh, stimulates intense yearnings for what one lacks. One longs for a life, and if not the life one had, then some kind of life, anything but the living death of total dependence. Over and over, longing cultivates a readiness, sensitivity, or alertness for a way out. A way out does not mean a way back to the previous life. That life is over. Rather, it means concretely any tangible improvement in one's situation that suggests a difference in the life to be lived. One is trapped in a world in which most of what made life worthwhile is gone, and threatened by the possibility that his bleak existence might extend indefinitely into the future. Overwhelmed, a person might retreat to fantasy, false hopes, and distractions, or try to numb oneself to living (e.g., drugs, alcohol). However, if the agony of experiencing the gap in its diverse forms (e.g., depression) has been allowed to function properly, a person is inspired to seek a way out, to search for realistic possibilities for improvement.

Positioning

A sense of incompleteness is not so much left behind as incorporated in the next phase, supplying a continuing basis for striving.

Escape begins with the formation of a goal, but not just any goal. For example, during incompleteness, Ray tried to will his legs to move, no doubt with the hope that he would regain movement and eventually leave that bed to begin life as before. It was a false hope, dooming efforts to futility. In the beginning, it is not clear what is possible and one must explore, gain information on one's condition. The kind of goal that moves a person from incompleteness is one that seems "real" and attainable, one that marks an improvement of one's condition and a movement away from dependence. When meaning in life has virtually collapsed to the prospect of improvement, such a goal takes on a salvational significance.

While a person begins the pursuit of a goal because of its meaningfulness, maintaining that pursuit requires other critical features. First, it is better if a goal is specific and definite for the person can then monitor progress and establish standards for success. For example, breathing without a ventilator for two minutes is quite definite. One can monitor progress and know when the goal is reached. Second, taking ownership for a goal seems crucial, and was particularly noted in Tom's account. It involves a recognition that pursuing a goal is self-determined; it depends on oneself, one's own willingness to strive. This recognition contrasts with other experiences in which one is manipulated or acted on. While this self-determined character of goal setting seems to naturally expand into a conviction that one can make a difference or affect outcomes through effort, one is initially uncertain of having an impact. It is not clear what one is capable or incapable of doing.

The soaring moments of this phase are experiences of success. In part, success invigorates the pattern of striving to reach goals, validating one's capacity to make a difference. In part, success validates a more hopeful future. Thus, Ray and Tom report not just exhilaration, but also feelings of freedom, independence, and control. Success encourages or inspires confidence in present tasks and in a more agentic plot for future efforts. However, successes occur more as one goes along. Beginning efforts are apt to be faltering, filled with obstacles and setbacks. In short, confidence (efficacy, internal locus of control) grows over time, strongly supporting the pursuit of goals, but it does not appear to be salient at the beginning.

Pursuing goals reorganizes life. The life of a patient feels empty. Having things to do that are meaningful fills life with purpose. Time becomes structured by anticipations and evaluations, plans and preparations. Other people and settings become cast as facilitations or hindrances. Pursuing goals essentially creates a dramatization in which situations become defined, roles are aligned, role ideals are constructed and purposes clarified. In this drama, one is learning to enact the role of an agent, composing a more agentic orientation to guide striving.

Composition of an agentic plot is elaborated by experiences that indicate a staying on course or going off course. For example, one might learn to both accept and reject advice, realizing that it is the role of advice in moving plans along that matters. That is, it is not agentic to just reject advice as if rejection implied independence. Rather, an agent must consider the value of advice and decide. As another example, negative models might vividly portray contrasting plots to avoid. One learns by opposing implications, becoming what the negative model is not. Through these kinds of experiences, scenarios are added to the basic plot of striving to reach a goal, providing a fuller repertoire of ways to stay on course within the confusions of everyday life.

A person leaves this phase when he or she is finally in position or prepared. That is, there are opportunities that a person is capable of pursuing. For example, Tom could not counsel others very well until he could breathe on his own to talk. And he could not counsel others without the opportunity to do so and the willingness to try. For Ray, the decisive change was movement to a new setting, leaving a medical facility and going home. In these "real-world" opportunities, all the efforts of positioning come to a point.

Actualizing

During this phase, practice continues, but instead of remaining the figure of existence, becomes a supportive ground for engaging in meaningful activities, recovering a life. The shift is analogous to the difference between practicing for a big game and actually playing that game. More seems to be at stake. It seems more real. What the person seeks is to transform potentials into actualities.

As the person begins, he or she does not know what is possible. There are numerous wants such as friends, status, fun, romance, worthwhile activities, and so on, but no way of knowing what is possible or impossible. One must explore, wait and see, try things out. There is no plan really, but more of a readiness to act on what one can. As opportunities arise, the person acts (often with misgivings). Through involvement in one activity, other opportunities arise. In this way, a person's life begins to fill with roles, relationships, and activities.

The rapid expansion of life increasingly calls for broader evaluation. First, the person becomes aware that the major barriers to fuller and more enjoyable participation in activities stem from one's own beliefs and attitudes, particularly those concerned with oneself. In different ways, individuals question their frames for negative evaluation, the basis for judging themselves primarily by weaknesses. Each person eventually establishes a broader basis for self-evaluation, one in which strengths might be seen and appreciated. From this new perspective, they emerge as more worthy and competent persons. In short, each person recasts his or her role in life. Second, as life fills up and seems likely to expand further, a person becomes aware that life is being shaped or taking on a certain shape. One begins to question that life from various angles. Do I like my life? How much more can I recover? Through this questioning, standing back and evaluating, a person becomes more aware that opportunities require decisions, and decisions require an understanding of what one wants from life. In this way, a person becomes more active in shaping life, more clear about the future plot of life that is to unfold.

Toward the second half of this phase, the person is much more active as a center of control and decision. Regarding oneself, there are personal qualities to cultivate or suppress. Regarding situations, there are roles, relationships, and activities to cultivate, neglect, or reject (perhaps leave behind). Through plans and purposes of a broader view of one's present and future, life is being authored. While agentic features were central during positioning, they are now incorporated as parts of a more individuated character. For example, confidence might fit with sensitivity (one quality strongly agentic and the other possibly so) in forming a more unifying self-definition. Successes are no longer merely agentic experiences, but also consolidations of identity, self-legislated engagements that indicate the kinds of values that are to prevail in one's life.

Completion

A person emerges from the phase of actualizing with the realization that oneself and one's life are complete. No unrealistic criteria are desirable here for completion lies in the person's sense of life, feelings and attitudes. It is only a relative completion, a counterpoint to living always with a sense of lack. Now, one lives with a sense of life being on course, full, open to possibilities or unrestricted. Within the bounds of one's disability, a person has achieved a sense of wholeness that is not chronically spoiled by what once was, one's perceived deficits, self-devaluation, or physical reminders of being disabled. In short, a person becomes vividly aware of what positively is.

This newly found sense of possibility seems to be consolidated by memorable experiences that portray the person one now is, the life one has. These experiences serve as prototypical plots that help guide future courses of action, crystallizing what it is to be an agent of one's career. Further, the plot of these experiences reflects the story of one's recovery, offering a continuity to one's life history. For the person, these culminating experiences radiate with meaning, a meaning that can be reexperienced with each telling to warn, console, inspire, or direct as one engages future difficulties and opportunities.

Commentary

In this attempt to construct a pattern from concrete accounts of rehabilitation, the major claims of agency theorists are quite evident. Core features such as purposefulness, confidence, and self-determination are not just present, but pivotal in moving the story along. However, a story also portrays context, and within the shifting contexts, features of agency play different roles and have special times of significance. In short, while important propositions (e.g., success enhances self-efficacy or confidence) seem amply demonstrated, they are also qualified by context.

One qualification is temporal. Theoretical propositions tend to be stated in a timeless fashion while concrete accounts embed these propositions in a temporal course. For example, according to

Bandura (1989), the mark of an efficacious person is perseverance in the face of obstacles and setbacks, and this perseverance stems from a belief that one is capable of successfully completing tasks or executing courses of action to deal with situations. Thus, we expect perseverance when a person believes he or she can make a difference and faltering when one believes he or she cannot make a difference. However, both Ray and Tom persevered before they felt efficacious. Both were uncertain, and in their situations, uncertainty was very close to hope. Nor did either person experience much success at the beginning. Rather, they experienced more obstacles, setbacks, and failures; only later was success experienced with more frequency. When they did experience success and came to believe they could make a difference, the result was as expected. Vigorous, determined effort was supported.

As another illustration, consider the power of negative models in Ray's account. They represented the dreaded possibility of being broken, and inspired Ray to strive even harder to achieve goals, to separate himself from them. Positive models did not appear until much later. While this might be fortuitous, it seems more likely that the significance of models depends upon context. For example, as a general pattern, the negative is fully experienced and clarified first, stimulating yearning for the positive which is gradually experienced and clarified later. One first seeks escape or freedom from and later moves toward "freedom to." Consequently, negative models would help clarify the negative at the beginning, but might be irrelevant or much less important later. Positive models are important in clarifying possibilities, but might be difficult to accept or react constructively to early on. The context or situation of the person (which we have attempted to order in four phases) seems to provide a strong influence on what agentic principles and events are apt to be relevant or important, and salience varies across contexts.

A second qualification concerns function in story. For example, during the actualizing phase, an important development is that the person broadens and revises his or her basis for self-evaluation. As a physical being, one remains a cripple. As a person, there are a broader range of virtues. For Ray, this reconstruction was greatly facilitated by a relationship. For Tom, it was facilitated by religion. Both played a similar role in story. Each might also have played a different role in story. Indeed, both the relationship and the religion contributed to other developments; whether a particular such as a model or an event such as success, each stands as an open possibility in story that cannot definitely by fixed, except perhaps in retrospect. Thus, one might encounter models that have little impact, models that inspire or breed despair, models that enhance confidence or undermine confidence, and so on. It is not the sheer fact of having a model available that is the proper level for understanding, but the functions of that model in forwarding the plot.

A final qualification concerns the configuration of agentic features. For example, what supported perseverance in early efforts? In the absence of confidence, something else supported determined effort and that something else might vary from case to case. It appears that having explored total dependency and found it void of meaning, any possibility suggestive of progress became incredibly meaningful. Thus, one might say that one feature fills in for another in a general movement that eventually strengthens all the features. Yet in coordinating as they must (for none exist in isolation), each is apt to modify others.

Consider, for instance, the optimistic explanatory style of Seligman (1990). A strong agent is one who explains successes by attributions that indicate permanence (i.e., it was not due to just a temporary cause), pervasiveness (generalizing across people, situations, tasks), and personalization (seeing oneself as the reason for success), while explaining failures by temporary, specific, and external conditions. A patient is one who explains successes and failures in exactly the opposite fashion. By the way in which the world is viewed, an agent has good reason for optimism while a patient has good (but perhaps misguided) reason for pessimism. Among other things, an agent would view negative situations as changeable while a patient would view them as unchangeable.

Surely, Seligman is correct in his basic assumption that the way a person construes success and failure affects a sense of agency. An agentic orientation would involve attributions such as he described. However, as it stands, the explanatory style of an agent might conflict with other agentic features such as realism and responsibility. For example, at the beginning, Ray viewed his paralysis as temporary, trying for hours daily to will his toes to move. In this way, he learned that his condition was permanent. No matter what he did, this negative state was fixed. Accepting the reality of paralysis freed him to strive for attainable goals. By contrast, a blanket policy to view negative events as temporary, specific, and external would have encaged him.

Obviously, Seligman does not have in mind the encagement of agents by futile or illusory goals. Consequently, the explanatory style he advocates must be tempered by other considerations. For Ray and Tom, a major consideration was realism. Was a given possibility real? Could one plan to reach it? In a situation that was filled with uncertainty and prone to fantasy, they came to be almost ruthless in their exploration of reality. If ever they were to improve, to recover a life, it had to be done in reality. Fantasy, deception, and Pollyannish optimism were just other names for trap. Whether some condition (obstacle, possibility, etc.) was permanent or temporary, general or specific, internal or external, was not so much a matter of style as of active exploration to determine what was fixed and what was changeable. Without assurance that they were true, attributions simply lacked substance.

In general, the parts of a transformation in agency seem to have been well-marked by theorists. Agentic experiences formed the central thrust of the drama, organizing and reorganizing the life world of the person. Like a skeletal plot to which parts are added, these experiences gradually incorporated features of agency until they encapsulated an agentic plot of life. However, the major task is to enfold these parts into a coherent order. In this chapter, the order appears in these cases as a complex drama with four major acts. These acts or phases of transformation portray the general movement, but need to be filled out in more detail to understand the major themes of change.

4 / THEMES OF PASSAGE

Following the model of a rite of passage (Eliade 1958; Van Gennep 1960), there are two major themes of movement, progressive destruction of an old plot of living and progressive construction of a new plot of living. The aim of this chapter is to chart these movements and their relationship across the phases of transformation. Destruction involves detachment from, abandonment of, or positive change in elements of the old plot, increasingly leading that plot to disintegrate (lose its form) or recede into the background. Construction involves allegiance to elements of the new plot, leading to an increasing configuration into a coherent form that is lived. That is, it is not just a plot that one has knowledge of, but one that is enacted in the course of life.

Carol's Narrative

Carol is a forty-five-year-old woman, the only child of a working-class family in England. Her childhood was peaceful and she had a particularly close relationship with her father. As a child, she was a tomboy and played happily with her seven male cousins. Occasionally, she attended the Church of England. When she was twenty-four years old, she moved to Canada and was married four years later. After eight years of marriage, she divorced her husband and returned to school to complete a bachelor's degree in history. Currently, she is completing her master's of divinity in order to become ordained as a priest in the Anglican church.

As far back as Carol can remember she felt like an outsider. She was shy, introverted, and lacked confidence. She saw herself as an incompetent. She felt powerless and had no purpose or direction in life. Carol used to picture herself "on a boat going down a river with nothing to steer it with, adrift on the ocean of life."

Growing up, Carol experienced sexual feelings toward girls, but never acted on them. She thought that mother nature had somehow gone wrong, and that she should have been born a boy. At one point, she actually considered changing her sex. After moving to Canada at the age of twenty-four, she discovered "lesbians" through watching a movie. The two women in the film went to a gay bar. Carol followed suit and went to a gay bar to see for herself. She was not impressed. The gay bar scene was just like the straight bar scene, a meat market. She ended up meeting two women and went out with one of them for a few months. This was her first sexual encounter with a woman. The other one beat her up, and left her with a broken nose and two black eyes. Later, Carol found out that this woman was a violent alcoholic. She concluded that all lesbians must be crazy.

Carol felt she had to get out of this "phase" she was going through and decided to get married. She was twenty-eight when she married K and while she loved him, she found sex with him disappointing, something to be endured. On the other hand, being married was like a great weight lifted off her shoulders. It helped Carol to feel more normal, like an "insider," not an "outsider." Being married also provided Carol with a new identity, an acceptable social mask. She was now K's wife, a part of the "straight" world. Unknowingly, the more she acted the role, the better she got at it and the more distant she felt from her real self. When the marriage started to go downhill, she was convinced that it was all her fault. That's what K said and she believed him. Since she did not know what the problem was, she concluded that it must be because of her lack of sexual interest toward her husband.

A year into the marriage Carol discovered that K had a drinking problem. Suddenly all of his rather bizarre behavior began to make sense. She thought perhaps that she was the cause of his drinking. After all, she did not enjoy sex with him. He would tell her things like she was no good in bed and should go down to where the prostitutes congregate and get some experience. They would argue regularly, and K would manipulate and twist the conversation until Carol was convinced that it was all her fault. Then he would slam out of the house and go drinking, blaming it all on his nagging wife. Eventually, it got to the point where K would pick fights in order to have an excuse to go out and drink. Carol became more and more withdrawn and depressed. She felt like she had lost herself somehow. She lost her feelings too; they were too painful to feel. She prayed to God for deliverance; God would save her. It never occurred to her to do anything herself; she just felt stuck.

Carol regularly made excuses for her husband and told friends not to come around. She eventually lost all her friends and became very lonely and isolated. She gained a lot of weight and wore dark clothes. Her hair started to fall out in patches and she developed rashes on her body. She told no one about her situation, not even her parents. She was too ashamed to admit that her husband drank. On the outside, she had created this false sense of having no problems, of being invulnerable, but underneath she was in a great deal of emotional pain. She endured for six years. During this time, she worked as a secretary in an office.

One day, a new neighbor told Carol that she thought K was an alcoholic. This was the first time this word had ever been used in reference to her husband. Once he was "named" Carol felt cleared of responsibility. This same neighbor also suggested that Carol go to Al Anon (a support group for spouses and families of alcoholics). Carol refused, insisting that she should not have to get help since it was not her problem.

One Sunday morning when she was out walking, she heard familiar music coming from an Anglican church. The inner doors to the church were open so she went in and sat quietly in the back. As she joined in the singing, she was filled with a sense of well-being. The music brought back all the positive memories of her childhood. She started to go to church every Sunday sitting quietly in the back so as not to attract attention. She did not want the priest or anyone else to know she had problems. Eventually, the priest caught up with her one day. He invited her to talk because she looked so unhappy. She denied that there was anything wrong. The second time the priest approached Carol, he asked her if she wanted to carry the cross in the procession because the regular person was sick. She was terrified at the very thought and refused.

The third contact was to have a very significant influence on Carol. They sat and talked in his office, and Carol revealed the basics of her situation to him. During the conversation he kept focusing on her, saying things like, "What are *you* going to do?" Carol had wanted this priest to tell her how she could help her husband. He offered her a book to take home and read. The book was about people with self-esteem and self-confidence problems. Carol was incensed as she read the book. It had nothing at all to do with K or how to help him. Suddenly, she realized that she was reading all about herself; it was like looking in a mirror. Carol was shaken to the core.

Carol mulled it over the next week and by Sunday she had calmed down. She knew he was right. Somewhere in the book it said, "The only one you can change is yourself." She was beginning to realize that she had to work on herself not on K. After thanking the priest the following Sunday, she asked him what she should do next. He did not give her an answer, but again suggested that she try carrying the cross in the procession. Carol had begun to realize that if she wanted to change, she was going to have to do something about it rather than to passively wait for God to take care of it for her.

In the beginning phase, the negative plot of living elaborates and dominates. Trying to fit in and conceal her lesbianism, Carol entered a role (as wife) that was alien or inauthentic. As the relationship deteriorated, leaving her increasingly powerless, she withdrew from others behind a front of invulnerability, isolating herself with strong tensions and varied, agonizing feelings such as guilt and shame. Experiencing the orientation of a patient with growing intensity led to yearning for opposite conditions (authenticity, confidence, etc.). Thus, the positive or agentic drama enters initially as a yearning or hope, fueled by the negativity of living as a patient. Initially, these yearnings were general and vague, but as her situation became more desperate and she was confronted with mirrors of herself (e.g., the priest's book), the positive vision gained more clarity and definition. Indeed, she experienced the positive opposite in church where she felt peace and belonging, and recalled memories of childhood. The decisive shift of this phase was her decision to begin acting, trying to change her situation.

The next Sunday, despite being absolutely terrified, she carried the cross in the procession. While it was not a perfect job, she did survive. She began to carry the cross regularly and after a few Sundays there was nothing to it. That job led to other serving duties. Participating in the serving duties helped to build Carol's self-esteem. Even her posture improved. The church became a place where she felt happy and at peace; it was an escape. She felt a sense of belonging in church and could be herself there. In her marriage, she never felt like she was being her true self. She always felt like she was acting a role.

When the same neighbor reminded her a second time of Al Anon, Carol felt like she finally had enough courage to face all those people. She would go to try and find a cure for K. He would not go to AA, so she would go to Al Anon. She hated it and said very little. Each person in the group was expected to take turns chairing the meetings. Carol panicked at the very thought. After all, she was only a housewife and a secretary who had nothing to say of any importance. They suggested that new people attend five consecutive meetings before making a decision about whether or not to stay. Carol thought that she could manage five meetings, and then she would tell them that they were all a bunch of jerks and leave. She did not belong there.

However, as people started sharing their experiences during those five meetings, Carol had that same experience of looking in a mirror. She recognized that her reactions and responses to her alcoholic spouse were the same as everyone else's. For example, not wanting to leave the marriage because the person is sick, staying for better or for worse, and the like. By the fifth meeting, she knew she needed to be there. She received the same message that was in the book the priest had given her; the only person you can change is yourself. She knew that she wanted to change. She had to accept K for the person that he was or leave because she could not change him. The choices were clear.

Over the next two years, as new people joined the group it became apparent to Carol how much she had changed. She recognized in them the person she used to be. At first when she chaired meetings, she was terrified. As she continued to do them, she gained more and more confidence. It felt good to be helpful to others. She felt supported by this group of people and felt like she belonged, just like at church.

Carol began to think about leaving K and discussed it with a friend from Al Anon. She knew that she could not change him and he certainly was not going to change himself. There was nothing else that she could do in the relationship. If she wanted to develop herself she was going to have to leave. K knew it was coming; he could see that she had changed. She was starting to stand up to him when he got drunk. However, as Carol became more assertive, K became angrier. He started to become physically violent. One time, he threw her across the room. Despite knowing she had to leave, Carol did not know how to go about doing it.

By this time, Carol had joined a women's outdoor club and decided to go away on a women's weekend despite her husband's strong objections. Unexpectedly, most of the women who attended were lesbians. Over the course of the weekend, these women shared their personal stories. The stories were remarkably similar. Growing up and not fitting in, but not knowing why. Discovering the attraction to one's own sex, but not knowing what to do. Trying to cope by getting married, but not being happy. Carol realized that she was not alone with her sexuality, but this time it was different. These women were professional women (doctors, lawyers, psychologists) who were healthy and active. They were not crazy like the women she had met previously. "Perhaps it's not so weird," she thought.

Carol also started running that weekend and made arrangements to run on a regular basis with one of the women in the group. It was a weekend full of activities and lots of laughs. There was also much discussion about how women are devalued in our society. It was an awakening for Carol. There was a whole other life out there if she wanted it, which gave her hope. Anxiously, she went home to face a confrontation with her drunken husband. By now, she was just itching to leave.

Not long after that weekend they had an argument about something trivial and K flew into a rage. Carol knew that she needed to do something because he was becoming violent. She stood there thinking, "Should I kill myself or kill him?" She did not know how to get out of it. It seemed like she had to kill somebody to do it. Suddenly, a voice came into her head and said very clearly, "Pick up your purse and leave now." She immediately made a connection with an old Scripture from the Bible. God had spoken and now it was up to her to decide and to take action. She picked up her purse and left. As she walked down the street wondering where to go, she was elated despite the uncertainty. She felt free. She knew she would never go back. She stayed with friends for the next three months. It was a tough transition. She lost twenty pounds and patches of her hair fell out. K was eventually admitted to a psychiatric hospital and begged her to come back. After seeing him once for lunch, she was sure that she had done the right thing.

During the phase of positioning, her existence was divided. She lived two opposing dramas (largely in separation until the end). In sheltering or liberating contexts, she began to act more like an agent. At home and, to a lesser extent, at work, she acted more like a patient, yet with growing reluctance. Encountering mirrors of her situation cast her as a spectator on her own plight. At home, she was no longer submerged in turmoil, but could stand back and dwell on what was wrong. It provided distance, motivation, and a more precise understanding of how to change. Already, she had detached herself from responsibility for her husband's alcoholism. Now, she saw more clearly that what she could take responsibility for was changing herself.

Carol explored with the opportunities available. Lacking a definite plan, she entered spheres of activity in which she felt more at home and supported. In church, Al Anon, and an outdoor club, she experienced peace and belonging, found support, and observed models. With the negative plot still dominant, these contexts provided shelters or temporary escapes, but as her involvement grew, they promised a more enduring liberation. While advice, models, and encouragement were certainly helpful in composing an alternative drama, the major vehicle of change was the enactment of more agentic courses of action.

Carrying the cross was a progenitor of an entire series of agentic enactments, culminating in delivering a sermon. By comparison, carrying the cross is a relatively impoverished and imperfect enactment. It lacks the rich composition of agentic features that figure in later enactments, but it was a beginning. As primitive enactments of agency were carried out on progressively more difficult tasks, agentic features were added, refined, and elaborated to fill out the plot. Negative features (e.g., fear) were weakened and eliminated. As a participant, she enacted beginning forms of agency. As a spectator, she wove those enactments into a story line to guide further enactments, which in turn, would add further aspects of agency. The differential opportunities, models, and encouragements from sheltering contexts supported this elaboration of an agentic plot.

As an agentic plot consolidated, it became more firmly established as a rival to her old way of living. Arising in separation, the two plots came into increasing conflict toward the end of positioning. She began, for instance, to stand up to K when he had been drinking. To extend the drama of agency to encompass one's course of life, there are basically two paths. One can begin acting as an agent in encaging situations. Or, one can leave those settings to invest in liberating contexts. Initially, Carol tried the first path, but

K became violent and the prospect of changing her marriage seemed too overwhelming and futile. With this final realization she took the second path and left K. In this leaving, the two forces of the transformation were in direct confrontation. While the action is outward, it focuses the inward turmoil of tension between the two ways of living. For example, the positive side held out the prospect of a "whole other life out there." The negative side wondered how she could get out of the situation, how she could live. Outwardly, she left behind a setting and relationship. Inwardly, she resolved to leave behind a way of living as a patient.

After a short relationship with a woman right after she left her husband, Carol knew with complete clarity that she had been living a lie. The very secrecy that she had created to protect herself was destroying her. It showed her just how much she did not fit in the "straight" world. She began looking for her own place to live. She met J and moved in with her, and they quickly became lovers. Carol was feeling wounded, lonely, and lost, and in retrospect knows that it was the worst possible time to start a new relationship. Carol was very impressed with and attracted to J's strength and fitness level. J ran marathons and soon got Carol involved in weight training and distance running.

J encouraged Carol to train for a marathon. Carol had always thought that you had to be a top athlete to run a marathon, not just an ordinary person. J spoke of the importance of making a commitment. Part of making a commitment was overcoming obstacles. Carol trained for months and months, rain or shine, despite serious problems with her feet. Eventually, Carol did run two marathons (twenty-six miles each). She had come a long way from being winded running around the block. Carol discovered that anyone can run a marathon if one trains for it. If she could do something like this in the physical arena, surely she could apply the same principles to the intellectual arena which was an area in which Carol felt highly incompetent. Running marathons boosted Carol's self-confidence. She felt stronger, physically and emotionally. Now when she attended social engagements she had something to talk about. Before, she was only a secretary or K's wife. She felt like a nobody. Now she was a runner. She had something to talk about that was hers, something that she had achieved all by herself.

During this time, Carol switched to another church where she was asked to be the head server which involved many new responsibilities. Immediately Carol thought to herself, "I can't do it." This time she caught herself. Through her experiences at the other church, Al Anon, and with running, she knew now that challenges were scary at first, but ultimately they helped you grow and develop. You had to do things to change. It was no good passively sitting there waiting for God to change you. Each little thing seemed to lead to something bigger. For instance, being the head server led Carol into taking on the duties of subdeacon. While it was intimidating at first because the duties included assisting the priest during communion service and the vestments are essentially the same as that of the priest, it felt good to stand next to the priest and be a part of it all. It felt good not to be nervous anymore. The whole experience gave her a tremendous sense of well-being, potency, and peace.

On Easter morning Carol woke up, sat bolt upright in her bed, and blurted out, "I want to be a priest." Then she burst into tears. Somehow by saying it out loud it became real, undeniable. "It's like a wagon lurching forward, it starts to move and there is no going back." Carol did not know what to do next. She knew you had to be fairly well educated and she did not even have grade eleven. She was forty years old and had not been to school for twenty-five years. She talked to various people including a priest, gathering information about the necessary educational qualifications and the possible routes she could take. She received a lot of unsolicited encouragement. Other people seemed to know the direction she was going before she did.

Carol went to a community college to find out about attending. Having no official transcripts, she was required to write the English entrance exam. Part of the entrance exam required Carol to write a personally meaningful story. She wrote about being a lesbian. She no longer wanted to hide that part of herself. She expected to be rejected. Instead, when she picked up her exam, she was complimented on her courage and received a high mark. She decided to go to school in the evenings for a year to see how she did while maintaining her job as a secretary. The transition back to school was not an easy one. The same physical symptoms (loss of hair, bowel problems, skin rashes) that had plagued her after she left her husband, reappeared. However, over the following months, Carol felt very empowered by the positive feedback and the high marks that she received.

Going back to school gave Carol an opportunity to develop and improve her verbal and written communication skills. Communication had always been difficult for Carol. She hated social engagements because she had no social skills. She would just head for the food table. J had once remarked to Carol, "You stuff food into your mouth so you don't have to talk." The truth stung. Being in school forced her to learn to articulate her thoughts and feelings. She would have to do things like read out her papers or speak in groups. Learning to communicate allowed Carol to feel more equal to her peers rather than feeling intimidated and powerless around them. Instead of having no opinion, she was starting to have one of her own, as if her increased capability for communicating required more definite content to communicate about.

One day at work, her boss screamed at her and it was clearly unfounded. She responded by saying, "Don't talk to me that way!" He was incredulous at Carol's assertiveness. She walked out and stayed home for three days. The other partner of the firm convinced her to come back and not a word was said about it. Carol was proud of herself. She had not realized that you could stand up for yourself, say what you want, and not lose something. She thought she would be fired, but instead she was invited back.

Carol's newfound assertiveness had ramifications in her personal life as well as her work life. After five years, the relationship with J had become very strained. J was articulate, controlling, and aggressive. The way J dealt with conflict was to seek confrontation, whereas Carol's way was to withdraw. Even though J encouraged Carol to stand up for herself, she did not like Carol's new assertive stance because it meant that she was no longer pulling all the strings. By this time, Carol had seen J's violent temper, and her destructive way of dealing with frustration and anger. After asserting herself once, J had shoved her and Carol, frightened by her violent action, had fled. Carol wanted to end the relationship, but J suggested they go for therapy instead.

J and the therapist ended up not seeing eye to eye so after a few sessions, J stopped going. Carol decided to continue because she sensed it was important for her own emotional development. She found that it helped her to learn to express her feelings, particularly anger, more directly. She also found, after successfully resolving feelings about her father's death and a series of other healing experiences, a new awareness of her own inner resourcefulness and strength. No matter how stuck she was emotionally, she knew she had all the personal resources she needed to find a resolution. She continued therapy for eight months. By this time, she was feeling so good about college that she decided to go back full time and quit her secretarial job.

One weekend, Carol attended a workshop for women sponsored by the church. Carol saw it as another new challenge, another opportunity to grow. One particular experience during the weekend was pivotal. The leaders showed several short segments of film directed at guilt and forgiveness. Many people were emotionally triggered off by these films. Carol was not. After the films, people were herded into the chapel to "come forward for confession." People started to go down to the altar rail where they were met by a team of priests. As people confessed, they were weeping and wailing. Carol was extremely uncomfortable around all this emotionalism. She was certainly not going to cry and be vulnerable in front of all these people. After all, she had nothing to confess. One woman grabbed her arm and urged her to go forward. Carol snarled at her, warning her to let go. She was angry and was not going to get sucked into all this psychological nonsense.

Carol fled from the chapel, put on her running gear, and went jogging in the nearby woods. After awhile she stopped running, stood in the woods and cried. As she cried, she prayed to God. By now she felt like she belonged in the church and suddenly she felt like an outsider again. As she was muttering away to herself that she had nothing to confess, she realized that she was carrying around an enormous amount of guilt about two things, leaving her husband and being a lesbian. She still had not fully come to terms with either one. Few people in the church knew about her being a lesbian despite the fact that her own priest was gay. She knew that she had to get rid of this guilt and wondered what to do.

She rejoined the group and saw that people had moved on somehow and felt that she had been left behind. She decided to go through the confession experience in order to remedy the situation. After approaching one of the priests with whom she felt comfortable, she questioned the validity of confession. He reassured her and she decided to go ahead with it right away. They went down to the chapel. She kneeled at the altar and asked him what to do next. He told her to tell God what was bothering her and what it was she wanted to get rid of.

She told God what she felt. She let it all out. Carol had never been so emotional in all her life. She cried and wailed like never before. As she sobbed, she told the priest she felt guilty about leaving her alcoholic husband. After all, it was a disease and she should have stayed to care for him. As the priest was comforting her, he reminded her that her husband's alcoholism was not her fault. She went on to tell him that she felt guilty about being a lesbian. She told him that she knew it was socially unacceptable and that God found it unacceptable. The priest said things like, "God accepts you the way you are now. You don't have to change anything. You have to accept yourself the way you are because God does." After awhile, Carol was filled with a tremendous sense of joy and peace. She related these feelings to the passage in the Bible that said, "The peace that passeth all understanding." Eventually they both stood up and started to laugh. They both stood there laughing and hugging. Carol felt a lightness, like two heavy weights had been lifted off her shoulders.

She returned to the group and joined in, no longer feeling like an outsider. After that weekend, Carol lost any lingering fears about taking on new challenges. She had lost her fear of failure which was at the bottom of it all. She still felt nervous about a new challenge, but she would not avoid it or be overcome by a fear of failing. She would say things to herself like, "How can I be perfect at it, I've never done it before."

Also after that weekend, Carol became interested in the healing of psychic wounds and attended a healing workshop. The speaker, a priest, began to talk about the healing of homosexuals. He explained that homosexuality was a blocked channel. Carol was outraged, and sat there clenching her teeth and hands. After being told by one priest that she was acceptable as she was, being told by another that she was unacceptable was too much to bear. She said nothing during the lecture, but afterwards she thundered after him and demanded that they talk. She proceeded to lecture him for an hour, despite the fact that she was trembling from head to foot. They could not change each other's minds, but they were able to part friends. This was the first time Carol had been angry and had acted on it right away. Normally, she would have "stuffed it down" and it would have erupted later in one form or another. It felt good.

Later while out jogging by herself, Carol talked to God. She asked God who was right and who was wrong. An inner voice spoke to her and said, "Nobody is right or wrong, I am the spirit of reconciliation." Carol was shocked. Not only did she not know where this came from, she did not even know what the word "reconciliation" meant and had to look it up. She came to understand that no one is right or wrong, and that all God wants is for us to be reconciled.

Meanwhile, at the community college, Carol took a Women's Studies course on family violence and abuse. During one class, they watched a film. The instructor warned the students of its potential impact. Carol thought it would not mean much to her personally as she had never experienced any family violence. Later on in the film, a woman was being verbally abused by her husband. Carol quickly recognized this experience as one of her own. This was exactly what K had done to her, manipulating, twisting words, and blaming. There it was. Carol was trembling all over; she thought she had worked it all out. The shock of this sudden awareness was overwhelming and she had to leave the classroom. Over the next week she realized what had happened and calmed down.

Not having explained her departure from the class, the instructor was somewhat annoyed with Carol. Once Carol explained her situation the instructor understood completely. It made Carol aware of how easily people can misinterpret you if you do not share yourself. Before, Carol had been completely focused on and absorbed in her own experience and was very unaware of what was happening with other people. This course expanded her awareness to other women, and she realized that she was not alone and not unique. What happened to her could be placed meaningfully in the social context of a patriarchal society in which women were downgraded and often abused. Carol was shocked at the situation, and angry at herself for having been so blind and so unaware for so many years.

Carol finally ended her relationship with J after seven years. It had been coming for a long time. To Carol, J was just too dangerous to be around. She was tired of people controlling her and always pulling the strings. Carol completed her two years of college and was required to transfer to a university. She was terrified that her old physical symptoms would plague her. Surprisingly, they did not. Her marks, however, dropped from A's to C's. Previously, Carol would have been devastated, done nothing about it, and probably aggravated those physical symptoms into reappearing. This time, she went directly to a counselor. The counselor reassured her that this was normal coming from a community college to a university, and that by the end of her 2 years at the university, she would be getting A's again. And she did. Once again, it had paid off to do something.

While at university, Carol took another Women's Studies course. This one focused on women in religion. There were two men in the class. In one exercise, people were encouraged to share their life stories or spiritual journeys. Carol shared her experiences of being a lesbian in the church. One man talked about a subject that was completely devoid of any personal experience. Carol thought that was typical of men, not sharing anything personal of themselves. The other man, however, did get personal. He shared his experience of abuse at the hands of his father. He talked about his reactions to the abuse and how he became violent and abusive as a result of it. To Carol, it became clear that both men and women can be victims of patriarchy (although women are victims more so than men), and that it is the system that is destructive, not men per se. Men and women simply have different ways of responding to abuse. Men seem to get violent and act out while women seem to get passive and feel powerless, she concluded. Coming to this understanding diffused much of the anger she felt toward men.

Overall, the Women's Studies courses helped Carol to feel better about being a woman. For such a long time, she had wanted to be a man. For the first time, she felt content to be a woman as long as she was a potent one. She had had her fill of being passive and powerless. She also gained a sense of equality from these courses. She does not feel less than or better than men, she just feels equal to them. Realizing this helped her to feel more optimistic about the future.

Leaving K initiated the phase of actualizing, for Carol was then embarked upon courses of action to actualize a more positive vision of life. She was no longer just positioning herself for escape, but confronted with the question of how to use her freedom to bring potentials to fruition. She moved in with J, who seemed like the lesbian models she admired from the outdoor club. She trained to run a marathon. She increased her involvement in church, crystallizing an ambition to become a priest. As she became more involved in activities, her commitment and sense of meaningfulness increased. Free to explore, her personal orientation broadened and clarified. Supported by the growth of knowledge and skills, she began to crystallize an identity.

In her vigorous progress in composing an agentic plot and mastering a more agentic role, remnants of the negative plot appear largely as obstacles. As symbols of encagement, overcoming them repeatedly freed her from the old plot, characteristically experienced as liberation, control, and confidence. As quite practical and definite obstacles, overcoming them formed the pivotal scenes of her progress. She resisted impulses from the old story to stay on course (such as "I can't do it"). She left J when it became clear J was too aggressive and controlling to tolerate agentic changes in her life. Drawing on a history of agentic experiences, she talked back to her boss and stood up for herself. With a broader orientation for self-evaluation and identifying with others, she was able to resolve guilt over leaving her husband and being a lesbian, and to drop the front of invulnerability, recognizing that she did not have to be perfect to be acceptable. For each stream of activity, remnants of the negative plot arose, threatening to hold her back. Yet each occasion became a way to detach from the old plot, to decompose lingering remnants, and to affirm her new role in living. Each victory not only strengthened her sense of potency as an agent, but now helped consolidate her sense of identity as a lesbian priest, one who will help others through turmoil.

After completing her bachelor of arts in history, Carol enrolled in theology school to complete a master's degree in the hopes of eventually becoming ordained. Once again, she experienced no physical symptoms in this transition. In her introductory biography, she proclaimed herself as a lesbian which was a considerable risk given the church's views on homosexuality. If she was going to become a priest there would be no more hiding. She had accepted herself and so must they. The fear was gone. The course work required a lot of sharing in groups. Carol felt free to share her experiences. She was able to be vulnerable and open about herself despite feeling somewhat self-conscious about her verbal skills.

As part of the program at the theology school, each student was expected to conduct and to audiotape their own ten-minute sermon. Carol was reluctant to do this in her first year. Friends reminded her that if she could run a marathon she could certainly do the sermon. Quickly, she reframed the assignment as a new challenge. She was less concerned about the content of the sermon and more concerned about standing up in front of sixty people. She did all the preparatory reading and then just left it to simmer in her mind. She would write it when she was ready; she was not going to force it. She had faith in her own inner resources; it would come on its own.

As the time drew near, she became a little nervous and started to imagine blanking out. Suddenly, she realized that she was totally focused on herself when she should be focused on what kind of spiritual food she could offer these people. Once that shift was made, she wrote the sermon in half an hour. She took the assigned theme, "the end of the world," and related it to personal end times, when you think your world is coming to an end. She drew on her own experience of divorce and wrote about how leaving her husband felt like the end of the world.

Upon arrival at the designated church, she felt uncharacteristically relaxed. In previous times, as soon as she would get up to speak her heart would start to pound, her knees would shake, and her voice would tremble. This time she was waiting for these physical symptoms to appear, but they did not. She put her notes down, waited for the music to end, switched on her microphone, and began, maintaining eye contact with the audience. She forgot to tell people to sit down and when someone in the audience reminded her, she smiled, and asked them to be seated. She did not get rattled by her oversight. As she gave the sermon, her prime concern was whether she was helping anyone.

After it was over, the priest offered Carol some very positive feedback. He pointed out two individuals that he thought would have particularly benefited from her sermon. Carol thought that perhaps he was being kind, but when one of these individuals came up and said, "Thank you, you've really given me hope. Suicide is not my only option," Carol was very moved. She also received three written evaluations which were all very complimentary. Carol had never wanted to be a parish priest before because of having to give sermons. She had always wanted to do chaplaincy work. Now she was not so sure. Finally, Carol had found her own voice. Now there were many options open to her.

At some point during her transformation, Carol remembered having to go through a period where she needed to humble herself. Although she had low self-confidence and low self-esteem, she did not recognize that for a long time. Instead, she had elevated herself to the point where she saw herself as superior to everyone else. Being superior meant that she could not ask anyone for help. She had to be perfect. Humbling herself had involved learning to laugh at herself and to accept herself as an imperfect person. It meant letting go of the mask of invulnerability that she had created.

Delivering the sermon was a culminating experience, bringing to closure or fruition the lengthy series of agentic experiences that preceded it. From carrying the cross to entering university, the shaping of a fuller agentic plot seemed to come to a point. The sermon also marked a new beginning, filled with significant prospects for the future. Looking forward, a culminating experience is like a teaching story that inspires and guides. Similar to early recollections as Adler (1956) portrayed them, a culminating experience dramatizes a tested style of action. It unites agency and identity in a memorable course of action that reflects a course of life.

During the phase of completion, remnants of the old story still generated obstacles, but these were overcome with greater confidence and ease. The plot of a patient seems to recede into the background, lingering as a haunting vision of what once was and what might be if one falls back. It does not simply go away, but endures as a background reality that reminds her of the dreaded alternative drama. Throughout the transformation the negative plot functions as the antagonistic force of the story. The protagonistic thrust involves the formation of an agentic plot that is eventually lived rather fully. Even at the end, this opposition remains. What seems to happen is that the opposition changes over phases, taking different forms (e.g., obstacle, ghost of the past).

Thematic Dialectic

The opposition between positive and negative dramas functions as a kind of dialectic in which each identifies and attacks vulnerabilities of the other. In the transformation story, however, the negative drama is secondary because it is the antagonistic force that is eventually overcome. Thus, the form the dialectic takes is largely one in which the negative does most of the identifying and attacking while the positive must act to ward off these attacks. In contrast, the positive drama attacks vulnerabilities of the negative early on during incompletion and then becomes more devoted to building itself. Of course, this is only a manner of speaking. It is the person in a state of division who maintains the dialectic, supported by divisive experiences in roles, relationships, and activities of definite contexts.

The function of this dialectic is to strengthen the positive drama. The negative drama exposes and attacks vulnerabilities of the positive. In response, the positive drama works to strengthen and resolve these weak points. For example, Carol's immediate reaction to taking on higher responsibilities in the church was that she could not do it. If this negative thrust were successful, she would have retreated and withdrawn, suspending the development of the agentic plot. However, she caught herself and reframed the new responsibilities as challenges that might be threatening at first, but rewarding if faced constructively. In this way, she strengthened a weak part of the positive drama. Even during the phase of completion, in preparation for her sermon, Carol found herself dwelling on disaster. She removed the focus from herself to the people she was trying to help, allowing her to write the sermon in a short time. Again, she strengthened a weak point of her new plot of living.

Throughout the transformation, the negative functions to focus awareness on vulnerabilities of the positive, which Carol then attempted to strengthen. In abstract, the pattern is straightforward. If one is undermined by lack of authenticity, strengthen authenticity. If one is threatened by incompetence, strengthen competence. And so on. Lacks become the focus for improvement. Across cases, there is a general principle of prudence in these engagements: Do not become overwhelmed. Taking risks and accepting challenges are advocated, but not excessive risks or overwhelming challenges. Within the flow of the transformation story, this prudential principle makes considerable sense, for if one is overwhelmed and loses the engagement, the vulnerability becomes even worse and the negative drama is strengthened. The prudential principle is a rule of conduct to make the dialectic manageable and fruitful.

What guides the dialectic? The prudential principle offers a major consideration that concerns readiness and selectivity, but does not go far enough to account for pattern. Within a transformation story, there are many factors that could influence the kinds of battles to be fought, but would not necessarily yield a coherent dialectic of development. That is, one could engage in fragmented, piecemeal, and scattered contests between positive and negative dramas, contests that appear chaotic rather than ordered. Given the contingent circumstances in which people exist, a good case could be made for random, chaotic clashes. For example, other people are often antagonists and they might be said to determine the nature and order of clashes. Settings involve rules and roles that obstruct some actions and facilitate others, encourage some qualities and discourage others, and they might determine the nature of clashes. In short, there are powerful rivals to the claim that a dialectic is directed in a personal order, yet it seems apparent in the three cases thus far that there was such an order. Now, what might account for it? What aspects of a person establish and maintain an order in the dialectic?

Beth's Narrative

Beth is a forty-six-year-old woman, the second oldest of six children from a working-class family. At age seventeen, she married and eighteen years later, was divorced. She has a master's degree in school psychology and is completing a doctorate in educational psychology. Currently, she works as a school psychologist for a school board and as a counselor in a university counseling center.

Beth's father was an alcoholic. He was authoritarian, rigid, and domineering. He was physically abusive toward Beth and would beat her for just about any reason, like being ten minutes late or showing any kind of independent behavior. Beth's father was also emotionally abusive. The only emotion he ever showed was anger. He belittled and berated her, making sure she understood that females were of no value whatsoever, and that she had no right to ever question or disagree with his authority. Beth lived in constant fear and anxiety. Like her mother, she tried harder and harder to please her father in order to gain his acceptance and approval. It did not seem to matter what she said or did, nothing made any difference.

Beth's father told her that until she was twenty-one, she had to do exactly what he said. At age twenty-one, she would be free to do as she liked, but not before. At eight years old, twenty-one was more than twice her lifetime away. She felt hopeless and part of her wanted to die. The other part of her wanted to live because someday she would be free. She vowed that once freed from her father's tyranny, she would never allow anyone to tell her what to do again. Until she was free, she had to develop ways to survive. She learned to never disagree with him and to never fight back. She also learned to lie fluently about what she thought, what she felt, and what she did. She lived life as a kind of impostor never showing her real self to her father.

Beth's memories of her school years are sparse. One memory that stands out clearly was an interaction with a math teacher. In class one day, Mr. H told Beth that she was special and had a lot of potential. He encouraged her to do something important with it. His words were very important because she had never received any support or encouragement from any other man. The fact that Mr. H reminded Beth of her father and was telling her that she was worth something made it even more significant. Beth felt empowered by his words. For many years to come, those words would keep coming back to Beth. As it turned out, Beth's father would not allow her to leave home to go away to university, so she lost interest in school, quit and went to work in a bank. She focused her attention on her boyfriend, R, who was dynamic and exciting. Beth got pregnant at seventeen, married R, and later had a miscarriage.

Getting married at seventeen was an early escape from her father's prison, or so Beth thought. In her job at the bank, Beth perceived her work environment as unfair and unjust.

She soon became aware that men in the bank were paid more, started in higher positions, and were promoted more quickly than women. Beth was an experienced teller, and she would train and supervise men starting out. Within months, they would be supervising her. She began talking about her perceptions to other women in the bank, and was soon called into the boss's office. He told her that she was misguided to believe that women deserved the same rights as men. Beth was both afraid and angered by this man's attitude. He was talking just like her father, but at least she knew that he could not hit her. With this knowledge, she wanted to fight back. She refused to stay silent about the injustice she saw. For so many years, she had been forced to stay silent. She might lose her job, but it would be worth it to fight back and say how she really felt. After speaking her mind, she felt strong and proud.

Beth told R about the incident and instead of offering his support, he called her "an impudent little punk." He demanded to know who she thought she was talking to her boss in that way. Beth was horrified by what she heard. She realized that she had married a man with views not unlike her father's. At the time, she chose to deny the significance of this realization. Part of her denial was related to the circumstances she found herself in; she was pregnant and married to a man she was deeply in love with. She felt trapped, devastated, and alone. Eventually after being passed over for promotion again, she left the bank and the work force to become a full-time mother. By this time, she had had two sons. Later, she returned to work as a bookkeeper for her husband.

As the years went on, R seemed to become more emotionally abusive like Beth's father, and Beth became more depressed and anxious. R also neglected Beth and the children emotionally and financially. The whole marriage seemed to consist of him doing and having what he wanted which angered and frustrated Beth. Beth worked hard to please him, but it did not matter what she said or did, nothing changed. To Beth, as long as R did not hit her and she was physically safe, it was tolerable. In her mind, things were so much better for her compared to her mother's marriage. She had no idea that things could be any better. It also became increasingly clear that R saw himself as the "boss" in the marriage and that Beth was expected to go along with all his decisions and plans. He was the important one. She was insignificant. Any contribution she tried to make was discounted or downgraded. She continued to feel devalued and worthless, just as she had in her relationship with her father. Instead of backing down, however, Beth continued to offer her input and opinion. As a result, the marriage was very stormy.

Beth received a lot of disapproval from R and from both his and her families, for her noncompliant behavior. R would punish her by doing things like giving her the silent treatment for days on end which was very upsetting for Beth. For Beth though, in those moments of noncompliance, it felt like something real was forcing its way out. It was the part of Beth that was fighting to be real and not the impostor. She desperately wanted R to accept and to value her real self.

While one part of Beth seemed to be fighting to be real, the other part was living a lie as the impostor. Beth had learned that there was only so much of her real self that was acceptable to show to others. Being the impostor occurred in and out of the marriage. Part of being the impostor in the marriage involved suppressing the anger she felt toward R for the way he devalued her. Instead of expressing her anger, she put all her energy into playing the role of the traditional wife as she saw it. For example, she focused her efforts on making herself, her children, and her home as attractive as possible. Outside the marriage, she concentrated on being nice and pleasing others. She learned how to say what people wanted and needed to hear. She was guarded about expressing any contrary opinions. She created a veneer of strength by being a "superwoman" who was good at everything she did—the best mom, the best homemaker, the best hostess, the best PTA member, the best sorority member, and so on. She thrived on other people's admiration and approval.

One morning, Beth woke up to a shockingly clear realization. "I'm not living my own life. I've been had. This isn't me." Suddenly, she was painfully aware that she had not consciously chosen to be a housewife, a mother, or a bookkeeper for that matter. She had been shaped to pursue the roles of wife and mother, and to do anything she could to support her husband's career. She had participated in something that was now intolerable and unacceptable. Without Mr. H's encouraging words, Beth feels she may not have reached this point of awareness.

By the time this realization crystallized, Beth was twenty-nine years old and she had more than a decade to look back over. She had to make a change or she knew that she would be destined to continue living this lie. As she was getting older, she felt it would soon be too late to make a change which was a depressing thought. On the outside Beth had it all, a husband, well-behaved children, and a nice home. On the inside, however, she was dying. She knew with an unquestionable certainty that if she did not start living her own life, she would not have one to live. She would die emotionally and just give up. This new awareness was frightening because she knew that it might mean the end of her marriage, but it was so strong that it was simply undeniable. She had to do something.

During the incompletion phase, there were two major developments. First, from the negativity of the fatherly drama of abuse, disapproval, and subjugation, a positive drama emerged as yearning. Lacking the vivid definition of the negative drama, the positive drama gained definition as a polar opposite, being everything the negative was not. Subjugated, she yearned for freedom. Unworthy, she yearned for worth. Disapproved of, she yearned for approval. And so on. While vague, the opposites at least established a general direction, and when she actually experienced approval from a significant person, Mr. H, the positive gained more clarity and reality, an experience that could be retold to herself over and over.

As Kelly (1955) argued, people come to an understanding of their situations by opposition, establishing differences, and an ordering of opposition is one's personal construct system. Through the construction of a personal heaven and hell, the ideal and the actual (in Beth's case), events can be ordered by the experiencing person. While most of the events described in her account happened to her through the agency of others, and consequently offer the possibility of random happenings, they were not experienced as random or chaotic. The events were ordered as reflections of heaven and hell. The order stems from her personal construction of events, and what could not be so ordered, would probably be irrelevant.

In a sense, with the emergence of the positive drama, she emerged (albeit very gradually) for she could then take a perspective on the situation she was in. She could stand back as a spectator and reflect. Further, she became identified with the hidden self that could emerge into a full-fledged person in another drama in which she was valued and competent. With the development of opposing dramas and her own tenuous emergence, the ground for dialectic was established.

Second, her early experiences with father became a prototypical plot for the confrontation between opposing dramas. With father, she sought approval, but her efforts to demonstrate worth and competence were scorned as inappropriate. To gain approval, she was expected to perform in nonachieving ways, indeed in ways that were demeaning. She was intimidated into playing a demeaning role that she could not accept. It was too encaging and inauthentic. Thus, she learned to be an impostor, maintaining a front that was unreal while guarding a hidden self that felt real. Of course, the sense of reality blurred over time, swinging toward one side and the other, but the basic plot was learned and enacted, giving imaginative birth to counterplots.

The basic plot was extended, in work and eventually in her marriage, but with a difference. In both, she gave her opinions. She was overwhelmed, but at least she was exploring variations and possibilities, and she could always rehearse the ideal opposite enacted with Mr. H. In this episode, Beth achieved in mathematics and was encouraged for it. She did something that was competent, worthwhile, and authentic. And someone like her father had responded not just with approval, but with a recognition that she was special and had potential. On the other hand, she continued to enact the role of an "impostor," and performed so well that she was admired, yet this form of approval, as welcome as it was, threatened to permanently establish her in an inauthentic role.

Beth's experiences were ordered variations between the prototypical plot with father and the opposing plot experienced with Mr. H. Between these extremes, she explored, searching for a tolerable existence, but during incompletion, the negative plot was winning. Through winning, however, diverse defeats of a positive enactment help to crystallize more fully what a better way of living would be like. When she woke up, realizing that she was dying in an alien and demeaning role, and resolving to start living authentically, the decision to invest in a new setting (going to college) was not without precedent. It was but one more attempted variation of the basic plot. Her early vow to gain freedom from her father's tyranny was now being partially expressed as a resolve to go to college and start living one's own life.

What she decided to do was to go to college. She was going to make a plan for her life and set her own goals. Up to this point, her life had been largely determined by her father and then her husband. Beth also sensed that she needed to develop a career through which she could support herself and her two children, should the marriage end. Beth announced to R her intention to start college. He was outraged. Again, R asked her who she thought she was to think that she could go to college. He accused her of betraying him and letting the whole company down. No matter what kind of guilt he tried to foster, Beth's mind was made up; it felt like her life was on the line. Making this decision helped Beth to finally have a sense of the future.

For Beth, college was both a nightmare and her salvation. The nightmare part was trying to straddle both worlds. The world of college and her needs, with the world of home and her family's needs. Desperately, she tried to take care of everyone's needs. R was completely unsupportive and frequently antagonistic towards Beth's efforts at college. To cope, she consciously changed the direction and focus of her efforts. Instead of trying to convince R that she was valuable and worthy of his support, she channeled her efforts into realizing her own personal goals and fighting for herself. She simply refused to get depressed about R's behavior toward her.

The salvation part of college for Beth was learning and growing. It was exciting to discuss and exchange new ideas with others. Beth also met new people who were to become life-long friends.

In a Canadian History course, Beth's professor Mr. L announced to the class that twenty percent of the grade would be based on class participation. Beth was very troubled by this and nervously approached him at the end of class. She asked if she could write another paper or exam in lieu of the class participation requirement. When Mr. L asked why, Beth replied, "I have nothing to say." Mr. L responded emphatically, "Yes you do, Beth!" Beth's thoughts and opinions had always been worthless to her father and to her husband, so she did not think she had anything valuable to say. Mr. L's encouragement was critical to Beth. Like the encouragement she received from Mr. H, it helped her to keep going in the face of no other support.

Beth completed two years of college and decided to do one more year to become a teacher. Becoming a teacher was a practical choice based on the job market in the town in which she lived. She applied to a teaching program which ran out of a university in a city six hundred miles away. Two-thirds of the program could be completed at home. The other third of the program had to be completed at the university. After a positive interview, Beth was sure she was going to be accepted, but did not hear back from them. Eventually, she found out that they had lost her application. Despite her discouragement, Beth decided to pack up her kids and travel to the university to secure her admission to the program. When she arrived at the university, Beth demanded to see someone about her application. She was not going to leave without an answer. By the time she left, she had been accepted. It was an accomplishment that gave her a potent feeling of her own ability to make something happen. It was a glorious feeling.

Beth successfully completed the first two terms of the program. Leaving home to complete her final term at the university was extremely difficult because it meant leaving her children behind which she hated to do. On a visit home two weeks later, she was horrified to see that R had been seriously neglecting them. After a major confrontation and a near physical encounter with R, Beth returned to the university. She would not go home again until she was finished because it was just too painful and too dangerous. She had to stay and finish the program. Finishing meant freedom. After Beth's return home, she started teaching immediately. She had not decided to leave R just yet, but was now equipped to do so when she wanted. Part of her still wanted the marriage to work. About the time that Beth started earning an income, R stopped bringing one home claiming that his business was in financial trouble. Beth began paying all the bills.

R spent more and more time away from home. Beth pushed for more time together as a family. To appease her, R suggested a camping trip. A week before the trip, R announced that he could not go, making the same old excuses for himself. Beth planned to go on the trip anyway because she had promised the children. The night before Beth and the kids were about to leave, R announced that he was going to the South Seas for three weeks with a business associate who was going to pay the tab. She knew he was lying about who would be paying for the trip. She was not going to be treated like this anymore. An ultimatum just popped out of her mouth. She said, "If you go, don't come back." Having said it, she felt sick. It felt like she had been tricked into ending the relationship. At the same time, she felt a strength at having delivered this bottom line to him.

R went on the holiday anyway and Beth knew the marriage was over. While he was away things shifted dramatically for Beth. A lingering depression, there throughout the marriage, lifted. Everything was lighter and brighter. The anxiety that had plagued her was gone. She was free to be herself. She did not have to live divisively anymore, wavering between her real self and the impostor. Beth found renewed energy for herself and her children. So much effort had gone into playing the role of wife and trying to make the marriage work. Now she had all that energy to make plans for her own life without having to accommodate R. She was also able to be less guarded with her sons. Before, she had been playing the role of mother and had to do it perfectly. Now, she could just relax and be herself. It marked a new beginning for Beth, and an optimism for the future. R called Beth to announce his arrival home. Instead of rushing to make arrangements to pick him up, she quipped, "What do you want me to do about it?" R hung up. For once, Beth had expressed her real feelings and did not compromise them. She felt a sense of control.

The end of the marriage marked the beginning of a three-year struggle in the courts and a series of crises. For instance, Beth found out that R was a millionaire. He had cleverly hidden his money so that Beth had no access to it. Even after being awarded a one hundred thousand dollar settlement in court, she never saw a penny of it. She literally lost everything. Eventually, she decided that she could not tie up her energy fighting him anymore. If she did, it would prevent her from moving forward and that would give him power over her life. She forced herself to keep going, not to get depressed, and to not be overwhelmed by all the sadness and loss that filled her life.

While deviations from a prototype were explored during incompletion, positioning involves a strengthening and stabilizing of particular forms, plots that work. Returning to the kind of setting in which she had the uplifting experience with Mr. H, she encountered obstruction and belittlement from R. Unsupportive and antagonistic, R acted like her father. Only this time, Beth did not divert her efforts into defending her course of action and seeking approval. She stopped trying to convince a male authority of the merit of her direction. Rather, she attended to the task at hand, making a success of college. As she participated successfully in courses, she learned, discussed ideas, and made friends. Strongly securing her direction, she reexperienced with Mr. L the moving encouragement she had originally experienced with Mr. H. It was a struggle to maintain family and go to college, but her experiences convincingly demonstrated that she was on course. And when she successfully confronted authorities to gain acceptance for a third year, overturning previous failures such as voicing her opinion to her boss in the bank, she felt potent, exhilarated. She could over-come obstacles and thrive on the pursuit of her educational goals. She could make things happen and chart her own course, uniting competence with meaning.

During incompletion, the heavenly drama was mostly a hope, a possibility. During positioning, it was actualized as part of her daily existence. Actually living a more positive plot reorganized her life world. Having a purpose casts people, obligations, settings, and the like into facilitators and hindrances, supports and obstacles. In particular, she began to cast herself as the protagonist, the main character of her own drama, who could support or thwart her own goals. Bringing the positive drama into the realm of the actual, everyday existence restructures the way life is construed and expe-rienced. Prefigured in going to college, leaving R was experienced as liberation to pursue her goals more wholeheartedly, a kind of making good on her early vow to free herself from tyranny, and a natural extension of making the positive drama actual.

The order of the dialectic is guided by construing and acting. While she could not control what happened (e.g., being rejected for third year study), her construction of events placed them within an ongoing plot. Further, since she was more active, striv-ing to reach goals, what happened was now determined more by what she did. Similar to Carol, Beth's two opposing dramas came to be virtually embodied in two opposing settings, home and col-lege. At home, despite her efforts, she was still overwhelmed and lived a negative plot with growing resistance. At college, she lived a positive plot. During positioning, two opposing dramas are in actual existence (i.e., not just in imagination) and the dialectic is extended to action.

Beth decided to leave town, enter university, and complete her bachelor of arts degree in psychology. She had always wanted to be a psychologist. Now that there was no one else to consider, she could finally steer her own ship. She also applied for a job at the university to support herself. There were five hundred applicants for the position. During the interview, Beth expressed her need for the job in a sincere and honest manner. She was herself, expressing both her strength and her vulnerability. Before, she would have only expressed her strength. She would have said whatever she knew they wanted to hear in order to gain their approval and acceptance. When she saw her name on the list of successful applicants, she was ecstatic. She did not think she had a chance, but went ahead anyway and succeeded against the odds. She felt a sense of accomplishment, and a big boost in confidence. Beth knew it was no accident or fluke that she got the job; it was something that she said or did. Knowing this made her feel valued for her real self. It gave her a sense of potency, of being able to go out and get what she wanted in her life.

In a psychology course, Beth did a research project on child abuse. She discovered that physical discipline was the norm in our society. This knowledge helped Beth to understand her father's behavior a little better, but it in no way made it acceptable. When it came time to write up her findings, Beth experienced a "writer's block." She was overcome with anger. She was unable to produce an objective piece of work because she was being swallowed up by her own abuse experiences. She saw the block as a signal to come to terms with her own abuse. Beth decided to contact her father. She wanted and needed to confront him. She had had minimal contact with him over the years and during the visits she did have, she was focused on trying to gain his approval. Sometimes she had been so desperate that she did things like go out drinking with him.

She made three visits to her father, two weeks apart. With each visit, she felt stronger, revealing more and more of her real self to him. She was building up to the confrontation. The week after her last visit, Beth's father was killed in a car accident. At his funeral, Beth wept uncontrollably. Her body shook with anger and relief. Anger at not being able to confront him and relief that he was gone. The fact that he was gone meant that she did not have to fight for his approval and acceptance anymore. Whatever she did after that was for herself, and not for him.

Beth completed her bachelor of arts degree in psychology, a year after her divorce. At the graduation ceremony, she felt a tremendous sense of pride in her accomplishment. She felt more confident in herself, and was feeling good about achieving a goal of her own. For one fleeting moment, Beth thought that maybe if her father had been there to see this achievement, he may have valued her. Having completed her bachelor's degree, Beth decided to pursue a master's degree which she went on to complete in two years. She was able to focus completely on her own needs as her two sons had both moved out on their own by this time. By now, her self-worth had developed through her academic achievements.

The summer after finishing her master's degree, Beth went on a camping trip with a woman friend. As they lay in silence on a beach one clear, starry night, Beth was utterly euphoric. She felt so free. Her childhood fantasy was finally realized. She had made it happen. She had taken risks and had worked hard to make a life for herself that was better than her mother's. As Beth lay there reviewing her accomplishments, she felt pleased with the direction she was taking her life. As she gazed up at the stars, she wondered what the future would hold for her.

At her master's graduation ceremony, Beth was exhilarated. It seemed like the main speaker was speaking to her personally. The speaker spoke about the struggle to achieve and how important it was to do something with your achievements. Mr. H's words echoed in Beth's mind. Mr. H's and Mr. L's encouragement had been critical in helping Beth to move forward and to take action on behalf of herself. As Beth's eyes drifted to the rows in front where the doctoral graduates sat, she knew that this was not the end for her. In time, she would be back in this room sitting in that row.

Beth applied and was accepted into a doctoral program in educational psychology. She had achieved academically and professionally, but had done little work to rebuild her social relationships with men. On an outing with a group of men from work, Beth had a new and powerful experience. She felt valued and respected by these men by just being herself. She did not feel like she had to be nice to them or to please them, and she was able to express her own views even when contrary to their perspectives.

Back in 1980, near the end of her bachelor's degree, Beth had started a relationship with G. The relationship had progressed to a point where G proposed to Beth. Beth could not make a decision about whether or not to marry him. She decided to see a counselor in the hopes of finding out what was stopping her from making this decision. While in counseling, Beth had a profound experience during a visualization. The image was of her father, not as a big, strong, evil monster, but as a young, gangly, awkward youth. He looked vulnerable and unsure of himself in this image, rather than fierce and violent. Reexperiencing him this way diffused the fear that Beth still felt toward her father. By seeing him as less powerful, he felt less powerful. Beth realized that she was in control of the power her father had over her; it was inside her. She did not have to keep letting him block her. As a result of this visualization, Beth came to understand that her fear of marriage was related to her fear of losing herself again. Beth was able to connect the visualization with her current dilemma, and realized that she did not have to give herself up to G at all. She was in control of that and did not have to let it happen. After seven months, Beth decided to get engaged to G and ended counseling.

As part of her interest in getting to know and understand herself better, Beth attended an intensive week-long therapy workshop. She had two critical experiences during that week. The first one involved Beth witnessing men working on their own problems. This was the first time she had ever known men who were comfortable showing their vulnerability. She was surprised and comforted to see that their feelings were not much different from her own. It helped her to feel more connected to them. The second one involved an exercise with four therapists who each took different roles as members of her family. Beth's goal was to confront her father and to finish what she had started those weeks before he died. Painfully, Beth finally told her father how she felt. Through doing the exercise, Beth realized that she had been fighting her father in every man she met, including her two sons. She had been living in reaction to one-half of the population. Somehow through realizing this, she was set free. Soon, she began to laugh uncontrollably. She experienced a sense of wholeness or completion. It was exhilarating. She had finally escaped her father's grasp, and was free to live her own life in any way she pleased.

Leaving the marriage left behind the strong actuality of the negative drama. There was no longer a definite setting and a definite antagonist, but a memory. During the phase of actualizing, a person might undergo the negative drama in new settings, but these would be overcome or left. Otherwise, the person would return to incompletion. With the oppressive actuality of the negative gone from daily existence, Beth confronted remnants within her own orientation.

The dominant thrust of this phase was striving to achieve, and major ending points of achievement such as graduation became the occasions for strong spectator experiences (e.g., the camping trip and graduation speech). Remnants of the negative arose as obstacles or blocks to the positive stream of progress. Thus, the dialectic was ordered within the context of the positive drama. Blocked in writing a paper on abuse, she attempted to confront her father. Blocked in deciding whether to become engaged to G, she confronted visualizations of the negative with the help of a counselor. She attended therapeutic workshops to increase her understanding and further release the hold of the negative drama on her life. Unlike previous experiences, these were planned and purposeful encounters in which there was something to achieve and in which she could act more as an agent. These confrontations were reversals of the early prototype with father. Rather than withdraw in defeat, she wanted to win. Cheated from an actual confrontation, she eventually had to settle for a role-playing confrontation, but still the effort was one of liberation.

Today, Beth actively resists the influence of others. She refuses to do things to please others. She no longer needs their approval and acceptance. She provides that for herself. For instance, Beth decided to take a one year leave of absence from her doctoral program for health reasons. As she saw it, she got herself overloaded, so she would have to get herself un-overloaded. Before, she would have felt pressured to keep going because others may have seen it as a sign of failure or a lack of strength. Now, Beth makes decisions which feel right for her. Right or wrong, she gladly accepts the consequences because at least she is at the helm. As a result, Beth feels more alive, more optimistic, and more fully herself.

Now, nothing stops Beth. Her focus is different. As soon as she knows what she wants, she starts thinking about the ways that she can go about getting it, not about the ways that she cannot get it. No obstacle seems too great to overcome. Obstacles are viewed as challenges, not struggles to be endured. Maintaining her real self requires a conscious effort. She has to actively fight off temptations to respond to others and to herself as the impostor. Beth sees her change as an ongoing process that does not end here. She is involved in exploring and knowing, growing and changing. She is committed to wellness both emotionally and physically, and shapes her life around these priorities.

The end is extremely exuberant and no doubt overstated, yet her rejuvenation is clear. The account lacks completing experiences which suggests that she is still in the phase of completion, that powerful teaching stories are yet to come. However, if she stayed true to the pattern of others, the negative drama would recede into a haunting vision that would be invoked vividly during small fallbacks that remind her of what was and might be if she allowed it to happen. One would expect further broadening of understanding and empathy as she increasingly turned her attention outward, perhaps developing educational programs for the little "Beths" of the world. And in developing such programs or in directly conducting such courses of action, one would expect the agentic plot to overwhelm what remains of the negative, virtually a restaging of her transformation in miniature. In such a course of action, the negative drama provides a basis for the meaning and significance of the positive.

A Principle of Order

Despite the mixture of chance, contingency, and purpose that is evident in accounts of transformation, there is an orderly, dialectical development. That order rests upon meaning within a narrative context. Whether an event is a fortuitous happening, a contingent possibility arising from a course of action, or a planned enactment, it is the meaning of that event that allows it a place in the unfolding story or that requires that it be edited out. The principle that best captures the development of meaning through the four phases is the Gestalt Law of Pregnance (Fuller 1990).

As applied to configurations of lived meaning such as a plot or a full dramatization, the law of a good gestalt is that a plot will evolve toward as good a plot as possible within the circumstances. According to Arnheim (1986), the movement toward an optimal form or whole involves two countertendencies. The first tendency is tension reducing, a movement toward simplicity of form (e.g., symmetry, proportion, continuity). The second tendency is tension increasing, a movement toward articulation of distinct meaning, a fulfillment of the particular meaning of a configuration. One moves toward balance, the other toward completion. "Works of art and music were frequently cited in the gestalt literature as outstanding examples of gestalten, not only because they depend so obviously on perfect structural organization but also because they purified perceptual form to obtain the clearest and most incisive expression of the work's meaning" (p. 821). Given these two countertendencies, the Law of Pregnance is "a law governing the fulfillment of individual meanings along ideal organizational lines" (Fuller 1990, p. 117).

Following Arnheim (1986) and Fuller (1990), the movement toward optimal form involves cycles of order and disorder, resembling a creativity cycle (Ghiselin 1955). The tendency toward balance requires an enhancement of structure, purging the configuration of alien ingredients, distractions, and unnecessary detail. The tendency toward completion requires an introduction and enhancement of central features, resulting in some degree of imbalance and disorder. As a feature of the whole is brought toward fulfillment, it requires the countertendency to integrate that feature within the whole, stabilizing its structure. In this light, the Law of Pregnance is a law governing the evolution of meaning.

A negative drama is intrinsically an unstable configuration of meaning. As lived, its very negativity generates positive ground for revision. The negative drama is extrinsically maintained by barriers. Contextual barriers include such things as settings, people, and lack of resources. Barriers of personal orientation include such things as fear, lack of knowledge or awareness, and hopelessness. That which makes the negative bearable, such as a front personality, might entrench it further, although this is not always the case. In general, the negative drama generates restless exploration to seek escape.

A positive drama is an intrinsically stable configuration of meaning. It is stable, not in the sense of static, but in the sense of generating movement toward its own maintenance and extension. Given a positive drama that is relatively undeveloped, the direction of movement is toward the enhancement of implicit and explicit constituents, the consolidation of the whole, and the minimization, transformation, or elimination of unnecessary and incompatible ingredients. The dialectic is a major manifestation of this movement toward optimal form. Toward the end as the agentic plot reaches a relative completion, there is a figure-ground reversal in which the negative drama becomes ground for the positivity of the agentic drama. In this reversal, the negative drama finally has a place in the positive. As a rival drama, the negative opposes the positive. But as negative ground for the positive figure, the negative drama supports the meaningfulness of living an agentic plot of life. Without the negative, the positive would lose meaning.

Our claim is that the Law of Pregnance governs the transformation from living the plot of a patient to living the plot of an agent. It encompasses and makes sense of the pattern that is evident in the cases, as we have tried to indicate in our commentaries. Any particular event in the accounts might be satisfactorily understood by appeal to diverse reasons and causes. However, the evidence for the Law of Pregnance emerges most clearly from the narrative flow of events, not so much any particular event. An individual configuration of meaning evolves toward an agentic form, and the order is clear only when the series of plot forms are examined as a whole (e.g., from carrying the cross to delivering the sermon).

A person does not so much have a meaning as lives or inhabits a configuration of meaning. Given the structure and content of that meaning, there is a requiredness or rightness of direction moving toward balanced fulfillment (Fuller 1990). For example, when Beth was blocked in preparing her sermon, she was focusing narrowly upon herself. Such a focus is understandable, but wrong. It's out of place. The meaning of giving a sermon for Beth was religious instruction for the benefit of those to whom the sermon was delivered. Focusing upon what would help them, what was needed, seemed required, a partial fulfillment of the meaning of this kind of action. And it is precisely through such corrections that the lived plot moves toward more balanced fulfillment.

The evolution of a plot involves a lawful tendency, not an infallible process. There is ample opportunity for going astray. One reason is that a configuration of meaning exists within contexts that modify possibilities for development. Indeed, requiredness or rightness of direction shifts from one setting to another. For example, at home, Beth yearned for liberation. At school, she strove for excellence, among other things. If she had been trapped in an oppressive setting, such as she experienced her marriage to be, it very well could have curtailed evolution of meaning to but a restricted and narrow yearning for something else. In all accounts available to us, the power of settings was marked. Leaving and entering settings were major moments, usually turning points of the story. And the capacity to change settings is not entirely under a person's control. For example, to enter a medical context, one might have to be admitted to medical school. The power to leave and enter settings depends in part on economic, social, and cultural factors as well as opportunity and good fortune.

Settings shape a person by encouraging or requiring some qualities and discouraging or forbidding others. The influence of settings on the emergence of an agentic configuration of meaning can be quite subtle. For example, through the roles, models, opportunities, and rewards of a setting, some aspects of a configuration of meaning might be inappropriately emphasized or de-emphasized. In short, there is the threat of misshaping an emerging configuration, or of cultivating other configurations that confuse and distract.

A second reason is that guidance in developing an agentic plot is neither explicit nor clear. Individuals responded to what seemed required at the time, given the tensions of their configurations of meaning and their circumstances. They had no overall plan or elaborated purpose. Rather, one thing led to another. As they progressed, their temporal perspectives expanded and they were more able to integrate life around an overall purpose and life plan, but most of the time they muddled through with considerable uncertainty. Guidance often depended upon moments of intuition, insight, and impulse, none of which are under direct voluntary control. Given the contingency involved in having just the right insight at the right time or acting on just the right impulse at the right time, it is virtually certain that these moments could have turned out otherwise.

A final reason why the evolution of meaning is fallible is that it requires something of a person; it is not automatic. For example, realizing that she was not living her life and missed furthering her education, Beth had to act. That was what was required. Of course, she could have failed to act or having acted, failed to perform well in college, both of which were certainly possibilities. Either kind of failure would have hindered the evolution of meaning. Similarly, during incompletion, individuals could have denied or distracted themselves from the insights gained from gazing into the various reflections of their situations. Certain virtues seem necessary to sustain this gaze, such as wholeheartedness and sincerity, and it could have been otherwise. If so, the evolution of meaning would have been at least delayed. That the Law of Pregnance seems to be an evident tendency in accounts does not mean that it sweeps over a person. Rather, it requires quite fallible human activity for development and by implication, the rise of agency. Over the transformation, what is required to foster meaning involves increasingly more difficult exercises of agency. One must make decisions, seize opportunities, perform efficiently, resist temptations, and so on. In the balance is the capacity to fulfill requiredness of direction for a configuration of meaning.

Despite great contingency in human affairs, the movement toward good gestalt or agentic plot has one striking advantage. The evolution of meaningful configurations is self-corrective. Frustrated in one direction or at one time, requiredness arises for another direction or at a different time. The movement toward optimal form continues, increasing the possibility that mistakes will be corrected and barriers overcome. An unresolved issue such as Beth's relationship to her father is restless in its place within a positive drama. Over the course of her transformation, it was a chronic tension that preoccupied her, initiating many efforts to resolve. In this sense, the Law of Pregnance is a self-corrective tendency. Given detours, obstacles, and distractions, a flawed part of the whole configuration continues to call for correction.

5 / SCENES OF DESTRUCTION

In describing the progressive construction of an agentic plot that is lived, the negative plot has been portrayed as an antagonistic force. While this portrayal seems accurate, it neglects attention to the ways in which the old story loses its hold over a life. Let it be granted at the onset that the primary way the negative loses force is by the positive gaining force. Shaping a beginning, agentic experience into a fuller agentic plot one lives involves increasing detachment from the negative plot of a patient. However, there are also several types of scenes that seem significant in what might be called a scenario of progressive destruction. These scenes are notable because they are not primarily devoted to building a positive life, but to detaching from a negative life. Accordingly, we intend to set aside the topic of agentic plot construction in this chapter and to focus upon specific ways that the plot of a patient loses force in lives.

Emergence

Throughout the cases, there are moments in which the person in his or her encaging situation is mirrored. The mirror might be a book, a lecture, a movie, a relationship, a negative model, a turn of phrase in a discussion, or a workshop demonstration, among other things. When a person's situation is mirrored, particularly in the beginning, one is cast as a spectator on his or her own plight. In stepping back for a broader understanding and evaluation, a person temporarily steps out of or emerges from the negative drama. It is an intense, penetrating, and compelling experience. Individuals report feeling stunned, illumined with the force of a revelation, and moved.

It would not be accurate enough to simply describe this scene as a mirroring of experience for this description is too neutral. The representation encountered involves a critical, problematic, and broader perspective that stimulates questions, insights, and evaluation. It is as if the mirror (that's me, that's what is happening to me) penetrates to the heart of one's situation, calling for a commitment to change.

From an early age, Fay had tried to care for her mother, who could not reliably take care of herself. At age four, she was her mother's confidante. She had to be adultlike, so much so that she scarcely seemed to have had a childhood. In adulthood, she entered one destructive relationship after another, initially with men and then with women. Always, she was the caretaker, the pleaser and appeaser, the one who was to draw out the presumably wonderful person buried beneath the controlling, demanding, and sometimes vulnerable exterior of her partner.

She became involved with P and moved in with her because she was afraid of losing her. For the first two years, it was fine, but then P began to withdraw. Fay tried to reach her, to do what she wanted, but was ignored and had to try harder. She was being lured once more into giving herself up, when she attended an Al Anon meeting for gay men and lesbians that was to have a decisive influence.

At the meeting, one of the main speakers described what it was like to be a child of alcoholic parents. In a piercing flash, Fay recognized that this indeed named her. She had been the eldest and responsible daughter, the first of the siblings to face the alcoholism of mother. When the speaker described in pointed detail how she had taken responsibility for everything, Fay was stunned. It was a major revelation that moved her to a point of no turning back, much like the times when

her "real" self had seemed to pop out to cut an entangle-
ment. Once a real thing is said, it opens possibility and cannot
be taken back. Fay knew she had to do something.

From a mirroring such as this at least four kinds of experiences
follow that could very well be presented as separate scenes. Sometimes they occur as a separate but dependent scene, and sometimes
they occur all at once in one big scene. For the sake of economy,
we shall consider these four kinds of experiences here as ramifications or strands of a full experience.

First, from a critical representation of oneself in a situation,
individuals draw out or experience all sorts of realizations and
insights; if not immediately, then over time as they dwell on what
was revealed. Fay, for instance, realized that she had been giving
herself up in significant relationships, that a pattern of caretaking
followed from early childhood through current adult experiences.
It seemed to explain troubles that she had experienced in relationships all her life.

Second, mirroring often generates a questioning of the life one
has been leading, stimulating a broadening of perspective. For
example, Margaret lived under a strict religious regimen for over
thirty years, twenty-five of which were spent in a monastery. While
she strove for joyful obedience, she often felt rebellious and angry.
In seeking to understand the mystery of Christ, she found a book
that was condemned by the Church.

Reading deLubac was a shocking experience. It felt like blinders falling off her eyes. She could not understand what he was
being condemned for. What was he saying that was so
wrong? Then she read *The Mystery of Christ*. It marked the
beginning of a radical change of perspective. These books,
among others, inspired an opening up and a broadening of
what Margaret now realized was a very narrow perspective.
Before, Margaret was a very staunch and traditional Catholic,
a diehard. She was angered by people who did not uphold
the views of the Church. She did everything precisely the way
the Church said she should.

As she continued reading, Margaret began to rethink and to question things she had once swallowed whole. Gradually, she was beginning to think for herself rather than blindly accepting what the Church said. As she read various authors, it became clear to Margaret that the Church was frequently saying one thing and doing another. She began to question fundamental doctrines of the Church such as Immaculate Conception, the Trinity, and the controversial issue of women becoming priests. She found that as she broadened her perspective, she began to embrace views that were condemned by the Church, such as reincarnation.

Third, mirroring leads to or contributes to decisions, vows, commitments to action. Implicit within a critical mirroring of a negative drama is a desire to correct or improve. Action makes explicit what is already a potential in the way mirroring is experienced. Persons are repulsed, saddened, or simply upset, among other things. They want something different. Commitments are sometimes quite direct. For example, Beth woke up determined to change and decided to go back to college. Sometimes, commitments seem more indirect, stemming in part from the broadening of perspective. For Margaret, going to India was similar in spirit to Beth's going to college.

Over time, Margaret came to feel that there are many different manifestations of truth or God. She came to realize the validity of all religious, of all perspectives. There was not one right religion or one right people. It was not right to condemn others for what they believed or to burn them at the stake, which is essentially what has been and continues to be done. In her readings, she encountered stories about people's experiences of living in India. After reading about them, she felt compelled to go to India herself. She yearned to open a dialogue with another religion (Buddhism) and for a more meaningful perspective on life. Over a period of months, she got up enough nerve to ask the abbot for permission to go to India. Once again, she made a radical request. She was nervous about it, but knew without question that she must make the request or she would never be at peace . . . At fifty-eight, Margaret went to India.

Last, from grasping the nature of the negative drama in which one has been immersed and cultivating a broader perspective, a greater range of people to identify with becomes available. For example, Margaret began to identify with people from India and other "condemned" groups, just as her questions and views would be condemned. When she went to India, her identification deepened. "Her experiences gave her the sense of relationship, a feeling of unity with all people in all cultures. It gave her a whole new perspective on life. She knew with absolute certainty that she would never again allow herself to be shut off from reality, from the human condition." These identifications draw a person out toward a further broadening of perspective beyond self-referring concerns.

The concept of emergence stems from the work of Paulo Freire (1982). According to Freire, "any situation in which 'A' objectively exploits 'B' or hinders his pursuit of self-affirmation as a responsible person is one of oppression" (p. 40). The encaging experiences of a patient are, of course, oppressive, but they are not just reflections of a lack of character. They reflect real social conditions, situations, relations, and traditions within which people have been mired. "Only as this situation ceases to present itself as a dense, enveloping reality or a tormenting blind alley, and men can come to perceive it as an objective-problematic situation—only then can commitment exist. Men *emerge* from their *submersion* and acquire the ability to *intervene* in reality as it is unveiled" (p. 100). The function of mirroring, what Freire would term a problem-posing representation, is to facilitate this emergence.

Essentially, by representing the negative drama, one can stand back from it, withdraw with another vantage point. Developing this critical perspective through questions and repulsions distances a person yet more. As critical awareness and understandings develop through realizations and insights, the picture clarifies enough and inspires one enough to begin acting under a different awareness, making substantial one's critical distance and investment in other possibilities. Identifications are holistic reinvestments in values and ideas that are outside the negative story and embodied in others.

Rehearsal of Subjugated Experience

The negative plot of living cannot encompass all experience. There are always experiences that do not quite fit or are even incompatible with the dominant story. For Beth, the recognition and encouragement of Mr. H stood not just as an oddity in her life under paternal tyranny, but as an opposition. For years, she rehearsed the experience. Later, it evolved into the positive plot of an agent, but not all subjugated experiences do so. Rather, during the period of encagement and even later, the experience remains as a source of inspiration and potential orientation. It endures as a hidden source of strength. As long as that experience is alive, the person cannot be completely submerged in the negative story. One can always stand back, wonder, and at least savor another possibility, one that provides a glowing contrast to difficulties of the moment.

Near the end of her twenty-five years in the monastery, Margaret had a profound dream of a spiritual nature. Margaret did not and still does not believe in mystical experiences or visions, nor did she ever remember her dreams except for this one, which is as clear today as it was then. She dreamt she was in the chapel kneeling at the base of a statue which was on a pedestal, and she was looking up. Even though his face was unclear, Margaret knew with complete certainty that it was Christ. He looked at her and said nothing. He turned to go. Margaret called after him and asked if he would take her with him. He turned, looked at Margaret, and said, "Not for a while yet, I have work for you to do." Margaret did not ask him what work he was referring to, but said instead, "If I can't come now, would you grant me one favor?" He asked her what the favor was and she asked if she could rest her head on his heart. Suddenly, the image disappeared, and she felt engulfed by him. She woke up sobbing to the sound of the rising bell, filled with joy and wonder. The dream became a

source of great strength and courage for Margaret to draw on
in the coming years.

What makes an experience subjugated is its relationship to the
dominant drama of existence. Whether it happens in a dream, listening to a speech, succeeding in a task, or being swept away by a
painting might be relevant in other ways, but not to its status as a
subjugated experience. An experience is subjugated when it is disqualified or invalidated by the dominant story. For example, Mr. H
told Beth she was special and had a lot of potential. Her father told
her that she had no value and, denying any potential, would not
allow her to go further with her education. Margaret's dream
inspired a vow to pursue the mystery of Christ, leading to condemned books. The views in these books supported her experience,
but were disqualified by the Church. Since both sides cannot be
right in these situations, the subjugated experience is subversive of
the dominant story. Accepting its reality involves taking a position
that the dominant story is wrong. Taking such a position requires
separation from the dominant story, a stepping away toward other
possibilities.

Rehearsing a subjugated experience is a way to keep the flame
alive, so to speak, and it might serve a variety of functions in a
transformation. For example, the experience offers a foretaste of
what might come, an experienced solution to current problems. In
this sense, it is a forerunner of later agentic experiences. The experience inspires hope, initiates a critical perspective, provides comfort in stressful times, and so on. However, in the present context
concerning the progressive destruction of the negative story,
rehearsing subjugated experience is a rehearsal of subversive
thoughts, feelings, and actions that consolidates a counterorienta-
tion, one that endures as a potential that might flower into actuality. In short, it undermines the negative story.

The term subjugated experience was taken from White and
Epston's (1990) impressive treatment of Foucault's (e.g., 1980)
work within the context of family therapy. Basically, their strategy
involves three steps. First, externalize a chronic problem to help
people separate from the "dominant stories that have been shaping their lives and relationships" (p. 41). Next, identify vital experi-

ences that fall outside the dominant stories. Last, encourage the person to enact meanings from deviant stories and elaborate successful experiences into alternative stories. The role of subjugated experiences in the accounts of transformations supports the role White and Epston have described as a therapeutic strategy.

Leaving

The significance of leaving a situation (setting, relationship, job, etc.) is that one separates from contextual ways in which a negative story is enforced or maintained. Individuals can be trapped in powerless positions by threat, intimidation, authority, loyalty, lack of resources, institutional rules, guilt, and habit, among other things. In leaving, one leaves behind the concrete ways in which one has been held in check. With one stroke, a person becomes removed from the situation that symbolizes and sustains the negative drama. Leaving is fraught with both symbolic and actual significance.

Characteristically, it is not easy to extricate oneself from a bad situation, although it might appear so in retrospect. In fuller departure scenes, the person has to overcome a powerful obstacle. Ray had to retain a lawyer to help him to leave a rehabilitation center. Tom faced continual battles to leave the hospital for even short periods and worked for five years to leave it permanently. Both Beth and Carol had to stand up to their husbands. In this sense, leaving becomes an agentic act, a standing up to, opposing, and casting off of the negative story. While there are many variations, overcoming the final obstacle often seems to require determination and courage, perhaps stemming from sheer desperation. It is a significant experience that can be rehearsed over and over to mark one's separation from the old story.

There is also considerable variation in the experienced conclusion of such a scene, depending upon when it takes place in a transformation and the nature of the situation. For example, hospitals, medical centers, and monasteries were not thoroughly oppressive, not without many positive features. For Ray, a very helpful shelter had simply been outgrown and he was ready for something else. Other situations are more purely negative. When

Fay left her drug-dealing husband and his live-in mistress, her sense of escape was undiluted by any positive sentiments.

She felt free, huge, substantial. She felt like she could do anything, go anywhere, and be anybody. Sometimes she would remember herself in youth, so full of potential, and wonder where she went. Now, she felt reconnected, as though she had found herself again. Outside of the relationship with B, she could see what it had been like: constrained, narrow, stagnant, and awful. Inside, she had not sensed the full scope of her confinement and incapacitation. Outside, the trap was vivid, standing in stark contrast to her renewed sense of possibility, the sheer authenticity of possibility.

While individuals vary, they all seemed to be rejuvenated. Leaving was a kind of renewal. They looked forward. For those who also looked back, they could do so without immersement in the urgencies of their encagement. They had distance, perspective, and could grasp the nature of the trap much better. Leaving appears to be a pivotal scene because it provides relative closure to existence in the negative drama. It is not the last form of closure, but it is a major one.

Expressing Resistance

Having taken a stand against the negative story, however tentatively, individuals begin to resist its enactment. Of importance here is resistance that is expressed in action (things said or done). For example, one might continue to follow the plot of a patient with reluctance or resentment, but one is still following the plot. Actually saying or doing something is different; it disrupts the negative drama, actualizing a subjugated orientation that is not compatible with the dominant story. For Fay, a spontaneous expression of thought changed her direction more than once. In yet another relationship, Fay ended it abruptly.

When Fay learned that D lost her job again and that she would be paying all the bills by herself, she was once more startled by what she said before her guard suppressed it. 'You know, I think I'd rather just live alone.' As long as thoughts were inside, they were not quite real, but once expressed, they could not be taken back. 'Once a real thing is said, you can't take it back.' The thought takes on more substance as a pathway, a viable option. While B exploded, Fay packed and was gone in twenty minutes, another sudden closing of an enduring situation.

Resistance might be actualized in talking back, refusing to obey orders or expectations, or in more intricate actions. For example, "dropping the front" was a highly significant action for many of the coresearchers, one that usually occurs later in the transformation. Early on, a front is developed as a mask that allows one to get on in one's situation and protects a hidden self. Later in a changed situation, it becomes a remnant of the old story that holds a person back. As Fay stated, "it is a revolutionary act to be yourself." A person can become so lost in the various covers that it requires a breakthrough of understanding for a person to penetrate his or her own front. The social world seems to offer endless temptations and coercions to live what is felt to be a fiction. In Fay's case, part of dropping the front involved announcing herself as a lesbian.

All those years, she had struggled to fit in with a front personality. Now, she began to see a possibility of living more authentically. Before she had thought that if she could but see a way to live as a lesbian, she would do it. Now, she realized she could not wait for a clear plan. One lives life as a lesbian by just doing it, deciding and doing. Two women told her that she must make up her mind to either come out and be a lesbian or to not come out, but to make a decision. Fay dwelled on the decision, mused in her journal, and after two weeks, the decision crystallized, simplified. If you are going to be a lesbian, she thought, you are going to be one. There would be no more fronts, dodges, and hedges. It was really a decision to become undivided.

Seldom easy, acts of resistance require varying degrees of preparation and readiness. And some form whole courses of action. For example, Lee's father was brutally violent, explosive, angry, and when not punishing Lee with kicks, punches, and slaps, belittled him and humiliated him with such tactics as making him kneel in a corner when his friends were present. His father's cruel and erratic behavior left Lee in chronic anxiety and rage (He slept with a knife under his pillow, fantasizing an opportunity to kill his father). In youth, the main way he got back at his father or expressed a subjugated orientation was by stealing. Since it was too dangerous to express himself directly, he found sneaky, devious things to do, and one of the most complex involved building a front.

Lee tried to avoid his father's wrath by lying, never telling the truth. In this way, he protected himself. However, lying was another sneaky, devious thing to do, like stealing. It provided a way to also get back a little, express himself without immediate threat. Feeling unacceptable and worthless, the childhood pattern of lying became firmly established in adulthood. Usually, he fabricated stories about himself that were consistent with the person he wanted to be. While his lies seemed to make him acceptable to others, they also isolated him from others. He could not let anyone get close enough to him to see through the lies. As lying had become habitual, he no longer felt guilty (It was a way of life), but he did feel trapped. As he tried to become more of an agent, he felt increasingly frustrated and disappointed by his lying. If he wasn't lying, he was so emotionally closed, numbed, that he drove others away. What drew Lee toward a crisis was a deepening relationship with H. She was direct, open, and went after what she wanted while Lee was indirect, closed, and obscured what he wanted. She confronted while he avoided confrontation. H became increasingly frustrated that she did not understand Lee, could not get close to him or reach him. He always hovered to the side, detached and withdrawn.

The segment of Lee's account concerned with undoing his lies is included in total below. While lengthy, it illustrates the effort required and the ongoing context of change. While trying to correct his web of deceit, Lee was also developing and enacting a more agentic plot, receiving considerable support from others, benefiting from models, and learning to express feelings, a subjugated action.

Nine months into the relationship, H had had enough. During a telephone conversation after a conflict, H delivered an ultimatum: "Unless you take some measures to open up and do something about your feelings, I don't want any part of this relationship." Lee knew he had suppressed his feelings and did not want to go on living this way, but he was not ready nor was he willing to confront all of his lies and deceptions at this point. He knew that if something did not happen, the relationship was going to end. Usually in relationships, after a certain degree of intimacy was reached, Lee would end them to avoid discovery or exposure. Lee was sick of this pattern and felt he had found someone with whom he wanted to go further. He knew that in order for this relationship to work, he was going to have to make some effort. It was not going to happen magically. He was sure that if it did not work out this time, it would be because of his inadequacies and for no other reason. He agreed there was a problem and that he would do something, but he was not sure what.

Lee started to do some reading and some self-help exercises on his own. H suggested he get professional help, and offered him some suggestions. Within a month Lee saw Dr. B, a psychiatrist. During the first appointment, they talked about options. Lee could do one-to-one therapy, group therapy, or attend a six-week intensive group psychotherapy program. Lee decided to investigate the intensive six-week program because he thought he may be able to get results faster.

In order for Lee to get into the program, he had to stand up in front of the group (approximately twenty people), and state what his problem was, what his expectations were, and why he thought he would be a good candidate for the program. Lee told the group that he had two problems. The first one was stealing (his criminal record of theft charges was mandatory for him to disclose). The second problem was that he was having difficulty with intimacy in his relationship and he felt kind of dead emotionally.

Immediately, Lee was told he had to make a commitment not to steal. In some ways it felt good to comply. Having revealed to all these strangers the extent of his criminal record seemed to break the wall of secrecy. At this point, he was sure he would never steal again, and he never did.

Lee was accepted into the program which ran eight hours a day for six weeks. Early on, Lee told the therapists and other patients that he had a problem with lying. He was asked to disclose his lies and warned that lying was grounds for immediate dismissal from the program. They also told him that he must own up to these lies to significant people in his life.

Filled with fear and anxiety, Lee disclosed to H that he did not have a bachelor's degree, and later that he was on welfare and had a criminal record. The fact that H was doing graduate work made it even more intimidating and embarrassing. Each disclosure was utterly humiliating. Lee then disclosed the same lies to two of his friends. Coincidentally, Lee's brother was in town vacationing. Lee took this opportunity to disclose to his brother as well. Since leaving home at twenty, Lee had had very little contact with his family, and over the years had fabricated various stories about what he was doing. To admit to his brother that he had been lying to him all these years was very painful. The reactions and responses from each person were all very positive. They each offered their support and encouragement, reassuring him that they would not reject him. Surprisingly, each disclosure turned out to be a kind of a bonding experience.

The group therapy program was valuable in many ways. It set into motion the disclosures about lying and broke the barrier of secrecy. It also helped Lee to learn about his role in the lying problem. After one incident, he and his therapist dissected a lie to the point at which the decision was made to do it. This exercise was very valuable to Lee because he was able to clearly see that it was his, and only his, decision to lie. He also saw for the first time how complex a system he had set up to cover up that responsibility.

The program was also valuable in helping Lee to recognize and accept some of the rage he felt toward his father. There were specific exercises designed to facilitate the recall of these feelings. He dreaded these exercises because the feelings were so intense. Part of what helped him get through was watching another man express his vulnerability. Lee was inspired by him and it provided a concrete model for him to follow. Lee was touched by what he saw and he felt very close to this man as a result. He could see that showing vulnerability fostered a feeling of closeness.

The program also assisted Lee in being more direct with his feelings. There were two breakthrough incidences where he shared his anger and frustration in open, honest, and direct ways despite feeling afraid of hurting the other person, and in one case actually having strong visible evidence that he was hurting the other person. It was not until Lee did it, that he realized he could do it without being overwhelmed by anxiety. Even if what he expressed was unreasonable or irrational, they were his feelings and that was as valid as it needed to be. It gave him a sense of satisfaction and pride to be able to express these difficult feelings.

The program also offered Lee a fresh start with H. H began to see a vulnerable side of Lee with which he was very uncomfortable. He was not this competent, stable person that he wanted H and others to think he was. He felt like an emotional cripple. To adjust to not being the person he had been pretending to be for all these years was incredibly difficult. Going through the program was like going through a war for Lee. Without the support and encouragement of H, Lee does not believe he would ever have been able to take the frequent confrontations and the difficult explorations of feelings that the program demanded. He is convinced that he would have chosen a much easier route for himself.

When Lee finished the program, he realized that it was only a beginning, with much more to be uncovered. Unlike the stealing problem, he still felt vulnerable to lying. It seemed like lying was at the root of his other problems like his suppressed feelings and his inability to be emotionally intimate. He was still unable to be honest with himself, let alone other people. He still rationalized lies to himself and he knew there was still a backlog of lies to be reconciled with H.

To confront his lying problem, he returned to the psychiatrist (Dr. B) who originally referred him to the program. He started attending weekly one-to-one therapy sessions. In the second week, an incident occurred where Lee told H that Dr. B said something about the director of the group therapy program that he had not really said. H helped Lee unravel the lie, and urged him to discuss it directly and honestly with Dr. B. Despite feeling anxious and uncomfortable, Lee brought it up in therapy. Through exploring it, Lee was able to see that even though he had not been aware of it, he had orchestrated the whole scenario with a very specific purpose in mind. The purpose was to create a gulf between Dr. B and H, and the director of the group therapy program. It was a stunning revelation. He realized that he was not aware of sneaky, hurtful schemes that were going on in his mind. Not being aware he could conveniently say, "That's not me; I'm not that kind of person; I wouldn't do that." He realized that he needed to increase his own self-awareness and to take responsibility for his lies, whether he was aware of them or not.

As well as seeing Dr. B weekly, Lee decided to go back to school. Now that everyone knew he did not have a university education, there was no obstacle in his way. He could finally go back to school and do what he really wanted to do. After being accepted at a community college, Lee applied for a student loan. Within the first week of school, Lee was told that he was ineligible for a student loan because of criminal charges related to an earlier loan. H encouraged Lee to challenge the decision and he did. As it turned out, he did not get the loan, but it felt good to stand up for himself and to express his feelings, right or wrong. In light of the change in his financial circumstances, Lee had to adjust his plans accordingly. He arranged to go to school part-time and began looking for a full-time job.

H's emotional support and encouragement, day in and day out, were indispensable to Lee in his return to college. She also provided an important model for him. Lee observed H's self-discipline and watched her concentrated, focused school and work habits. Lee could clearly see that in order to be successful, one had to apply oneself in a wholehearted way. Previously in high school, Lee had only done the bare minimum to get through. H also helped Lee by editing his papers. Through her help, he was able to learn how to write better academic papers and get better results faster.

One of the required courses for Lee was French. French was pure torture. He was not good at it, and each time he went to class he had to confront that fact. He dreaded each class. It did not matter how many hours he invested, or how hard he studied, he did not do well. Frustrated and anxious, he persevered with the help of H's support. There was one time when he started preparing for an exam and the more he studied, the more he realized he did not know. It meant staying up for over forty-eight hours if he was to pass. At the same time, part of Lee's tooth fell out and he had a toothache. As he was still on welfare, he could not afford to go to a dentist. He called his welfare worker and asked for assistance. She told him that the only expenditure she could authorize was an extraction. Lose the tooth or endure the pain; these were the options. He decided to endure.

To cope, Lee developed a strategy. He made a commitment to himself to write the exam. Even if he did not finish school, but wrote the exam, he would consider it a victory. For three days and three nights Lee stayed up despite the fatigue and the throbbing tooth. He broke down the hours into minutes and kept telling himself, "I just got through five minutes, I can get through five more." He wrote the exam and got a C. Normally, a C would have been a devastating failure for Lee, but under these conditions he considered it a major victory. He was filled with a sense of pride at having persevered through the obstacles, accomplishing his goal.

One of the courses that was very meaningful and enjoyable to Lee was religious studies. The course involved looking at Eastern and Western philosophies which was Lee's academic area of interest. The instructor, J.R., was a very scholarly, articulate man with a wealth of personal experience. Lee greatly admired and respected him. Lee wrote his first paper for J.R. and received an A+ for it. Lee was ecstatic, partially because of the grade and also because J.R. said that it was as good as he could have possibly expected. J.R. also gave him positive feedback for the specific content of the paper and Lee's particular thoughts on the topic. It was wonderful to be good at something he was interested in. J.R.'s comments inspired Lee to work harder. Lee's next paper was a repeat performance. He thrived on the positive attention and validation he received in return. Hard work was paying off. It was energizing and exciting to get this feedback, particularly because it was the result of something real he had done, not something he had fabricated.

Sharing his achievements with H, and receiving her enthusiastic responses was almost as important as the accomplishment itself. H's support had played such a critical role in the whole experience of going back to school. For instance, early on, H had expressed a real admiration for Lee's creative writing ability. This kind of input from H was very pleasurable and helped him to feel a sense of worth, inspiring him to go on.

The summer after completing his first year of college, Lee finally found a job working with mentally handicapped adults. Finding a job had been a real struggle despite Lee's hearty efforts and strong motivation. Trying to get a job after being on welfare for one and a half years was like trying to get a job as an ex-convict. The other part of the problem was Lee's work history which primarily consisted of nonmainstream jobs. Securing a job was important to Lee for several reasons. It meant he could go to college full-time, go off welfare, and pay his own way (H had loaned him money for school). It also meant that he was a working, contributing member of society again.

Lee's job was a live-in position weekends and part of each week. At the same time, Lee now carried a full course load at school. The time constraints put upon Lee to manage the demands of work and school simultaneously were a major challenge. Essentially, all Lee had time to do was to work and to go to school, and it frequently meant all-nighters. Despite these demands, it was deeply fulfilling and satisfying. It was a challenge he seemed to need at this point in his life. He needed to prove to himself that he was not the kind of person he felt like he was when on welfare. He had to rid himself of that self-image and this challenge helped him to do it.

By the end of Lee's second year of college, he was seeing Dr. B three times a week. Seeing him was stressful and created a lot of anxiety. He likely would have quit except that he felt like he owed it to H for standing by him. Without her, he probably would have pursued easier options. The focus of therapy was still on lying. No matter how hard Lee tried, he could not stop. It felt like it was just out of his control. He felt helpless, frustrated, and anxious. His internal system for denying the problem was so well crafted that often he would not realize he had lied until some time after the fact. In trying to help Lee, Dr. B suggested that if he lied to someone, he should admit the lie to that person, no matter what the consequences. Lee thought it was a good suggestion and agreed to do it. This decision really turned the corner on lying.

The next few months were highly stressful and demanding. He had to admit to a prospective employer that he had lied on his resume. He had to admit to one instructor that he had plagiarized, and to another that he had taken a "cheat sheet" into an exam. While people generally responded favorably to Lee's honesty, they did not shelter him from the consequences of his actions. For example, the employer had said, "Thanks for telling me, but I can't hire you." During this time, H provided a consistent source of support which inspired him not to give up. When it was H that he lied to, however, the pain became almost unbearable because there was no one to support him. It was such an awful thing to be doing to someone that he loved and it made him feel utterly worthless. Lee disclosed to H as many of the outstanding lies from the past and present that he was aware of. Some of these disclosures involved deeply intimate revelations which were painful for Lee to say and he knew they would be painful for H to hear. Others were simply embarrassing like having repeatedly driven her car with no driver's license or having asked her for a character reference for a job when it was really for a court appearance. As painful as it was for both of them, Lee knew that H would not stay in the relationship if he did not disclose lies as soon as he became aware of them, as well as continue his work on eliminating them. She was willing to support his efforts only under these conditions.

For Lee, it was the first time in his life that he had taken responsibility for his lying. It was painful and humiliating to have to face his lies, but somehow it felt right. It was freeing to disclose them and not be so imprisoned by fear. "Being honest was liberating." Lee got to the point where he could not live with himself if he did not disclose a lie. Before, he would have numbed his feelings and said nothing. By opening himself up to his feelings, he could no longer ignore his lies. Numbing his feelings meant that he would be the person he was before, who was repulsive now. That was a person who was caught in a web of lies, who was isolated from himself and others, and who was unhappy about the direction and the lack of direction in his life. As the disclosures continued, the implications of the decision to admit them became clearer, and the lies became fewer and fewer.

Expressing resistance is an attempt to disrupt the negative story, to escape its unfoldment in everyday life. When the negative story is dominant, one characteristically resists other people, rules, and in general, external forces. As the negative story loses force, particularly with a change in setting, one characteristically resists one's own lingering contribution to the negative story. For Lee, exposing his lies was a way to undo his role in the plot of a patient. Dropping the front is a unique and complex form of this undoing. While most efforts to resist are quite straightforward (e.g., defying a boss), dropping the front can be a complicated, confusing experience for it involves becoming aware of it, deepening an understanding of its full scope and history, and grasping a way to resist it. Further, efforts to drop the front are not apt to be effective until one has developed a positive alternative.

Restoration and Resolution

From the cases, it is not clear if restorations are just common to some people or everyone. However, the examples are so vivid that it is worth describing what is involved. A restoration is an attempt to restore what might be called a lost self, one who was devastated by experiences of the negative story. In attempting to construct and master an agentic role, some individuals search for a precedent in their history. The search is like an effort to give their lives continuity by providing a new starting place. That starting place is an innocent self before devastation, so full of promise or joy or goodness. Perhaps a romantic vision, like Adam and Eve before the fall, it is real enough in effect. To found a new life in adulthood seems to call for founding a new starting place, or restoring one's rightful history.

Fay did not think of herself as having a childhood. The joyful, carefree, little girl who might have been had her heart broken early, feeling responsible for her mother's deterioration in alcohol. From as early as four years old, she had tried to support her mother, bolster her morale, do things for her, reassure her, and so on. One day at a workshop decades later, the leader instructed the group to "find the little girl with the broken heart and put her on your lap."

Fay spent the session caring for this little girl, getting to know her, and when the leader asked them to put the little girl back, Fay could not. It felt as though she had finally found her and she simply could not put her back. In tears, she told the leader she could not do it, and the leader asked her what she wanted to do. Fay wanted to take care of her life, a life that she was now seeing whole for the first time, coherently and without blinders.

As another example, Glen grew up with excessive expectations from his father. When he fell short, he was humiliated, belittled, and physically punished. Depressed and anxious, he gained a lot of weight and was derided and picked on at school. Alone and powerless he felt that he was worthless and deserved what he got. Many years later in young adulthood, Glen was successfully escaping from his father's rule and establishing his own career, becoming a counselor who specialized in disturbed families. In his graduate training and practice as a family counselor, he would sometimes become blocked, confused, and would worry that he might be hurting those he wanted to help. Recognizing that his feelings were getting in the way, he sought counseling for himself. As counseling progressed, Glen was shocked to discover that he had been abused (he had thought of it as something else and never spelled out the full picture). Overwhelmed and feeling alone, Glen engaged in a six-week restoration that changed the course of his life.

Over a period of six weeks, Glen began to take responsibility for himself, acting on his own behalf by attending to his own emotional needs. He provided for himself the nurturance he felt he had missed as a young boy. He did things like paint, spend time in nature, take hot baths, drink hot tea, and sleep with a hot water bottle near his stomach. Eventually, he emerged from this dark, lifeless pit of depression. He was filled with an enormous sense of well-being and joy. After what felt like a metamorphosis, Glen was able to relate to himself as well as to others, differently. He had found something in himself he had never known before; the capacity to provide for himself the things he needed emotionally. He felt comforted, more connected to other people and not so alone. He felt able to develop honest and meaningful relationships without fear of rejection. He lost the fear that he might hurt his clients and knew that social services were more in line with his true self. Becoming a doctor had only been a means to secure his father's approval and acceptance.

Some time later, Glen had a vivid, memorable dream. On a peaceful, sunny day, he was paddling a canoe down a river with other people in canoes all around him. At a fork in the river, everyone went down one of the forks, but Glen noticed something splashing in the water. It was a baby and as Glen drew closer, the baby lifted its hands up toward him. Glen picked up the baby and tucked it in his windbreaker. They did not follow the others, but floated off down the remaining fork, both looking out at the world together, very secure and contented. After this dream, he felt confirmed, ready to rely fully upon himself.

Whether acted out in an imagined scene or in actual living, restorations are necessarily symbolic for they focus on the past in relation to the present, the lost self of childhood in relation to the adult. Both Fay and Glen emphasized that it was a way to know themselves, to establish a worthwhile relationship to themselves. While it would be presumptuous to restrict these complex experiences to but a few lines of implication (e.g., one might argue that they rescripted self-talk, what they say to themselves), it seems evident they were powerful disruptions of the negative story.

Restorations appear to be a distinctive form of resolution. While restorations are infrequent, resolutions are common. In a resolution, a person resolves emotional ties to the old story. Even when the negative story is receding into the background, there are still remnants that are evident in reactions, self-judgments, and feelings such as loyalty, guilt, and shame. Since these remnants interfere with the wholehearted enactment of an agentic plot, individuals try to detach from them, undermine them, or in other ways, diminish their hold.

Resolutions took place in a variety of ways. Ray examined his reactions, the basis for them, and developed a broader frame of evaluation to diminish their potency and frequency. Glen felt guilty or ashamed of the person he was and focused excessively on what other people thought of him. Through a series of realizations (that negative feelings do not make him bad or worthless, that he had to accept parts of himself to change them, etc.), Glen freed himself from chronic shame. Beth diffused her fear by visualizing her father as young and vulnerable, rather than angry, powerful, and dominant. In part, observing someone else show vulnerability helped Lee penetrate through his numbed existence to experience and express his feelings. Some of the most dramatic resolutions occurred in cathartic experiences, perhaps because numbness seems to be so much a part of existing as a patient or victim.

To endure the negative story, individuals often strive to numb themselves. Not only might the potency of their emotions give them away, and therefore constitute a threat, but the sheer intensity of negative feelings becomes intolerable. To help deaden themselves, they might use drugs, prescriptions, alcohol, and wild distractions such as parties or promiscuity. Deadening oneself becomes a virtual style of life for some people (consult Peele 1983).

Don had lost all his friends by this time and his family wanted nothing to do with him. He had few visitors apart from drinking companions. One evening, an old high school buddy, M, stopped by. He felt M was perhaps his only ally. Don started talking about how he had messed up his life and began to cry. Soon his crying turned into heavy sobbing and weeping. He trembled and shook all over. This was the first time he had ever shared his pain with anyone and it was hard to trust someone. It hurt so bad. M did the best possible thing he could have. He told Don that he had no answers, but that he was willing to share his pain at the moment. It was a powerful experience to have someone listen and not turn away. Don felt exposed and vulnerable, but relieved. He seemed to have broken the cycle of numbing that had been there since childhood when his father died. It felt like a war had ended. There was no more denial after this point, just the raw, naked truth to face.

With this experience, what Don called the internal war was resolved. Before, he was divided, one half wanting to rebuild his life and the other half wanting to destroy it in alcohol. He would berate himself, try to beat down and overcome the hate-filled drunk he had become, but it had been a losing battle. He had lost his wife, his son, his friends, and any shred of a worthwhile life. Each loss had made him want to deaden himself more and to lash out, always denying his own contribution, blaming his descent on his wife. Now, the struggle was gone and he could see his life more as it was. From deadening, denying, and burying himself, Don now sought awareness. He began going to Alcoholics Anonymous and has not returned to alcohol. The cathartic experience initiated a series of resolutions. For example, he became aware of contradictions such as believing in nonviolence and beating his wife, or loving his son but drinking and driving with his son in the car. Resolving these contradictions stemmed from the loss of denial he experienced with M.

Other accounts portray experiences that are as intensely emotional as a cathartic experience, but are not really concerned with ventilation, relief, or expressing emotion. For Brenda, it was more an experience of hitting rock bottom and being utterly repulsed. The experience separated her from the self-destructive deadening that seems to accompany the life of a patient. In part, deadening is just a bad form of escape from the negative drama; its liberation is illusory while its contribution to further encagement is quite real.

Brenda flunked her second year of university. Around this time, she was feeling more and more depressed and desperate. She had started a new relationship with E, who later became her husband. E was emotionally inexpressive toward her much like her parents had been. On one occasion, they were driving along the freeway in the midst of an argument. He was being icy cold and she was crying. In a hysterical rage, Brenda threw herself out of the car. In retrospect, she knows that she did not want to die as much as she wanted to get his attention through doing something spectacular.

There were times when Brenda was so miserable that she pounded her head against a wall hoping to knock herself out. She could feel herself on the edge of a cliff wanting to step off, perhaps into insanity. Part of her wanted to have a complete breakdown, to be taken away and taken care of. She could not stand to feel anything. The problem was that she felt everything so intensely and no one seemed to respond to her. What she wanted was to stop feeling so miserable, not to die.

By this point, Brenda never went anywhere without a bottle of scotch. Not a day went by without consuming a significant amount of alcohol. She used it as a tranquilizer, to stop feeling. An employer asked her to babysit his three-month-old baby for the weekend. She agreed on the condition that she could have a party. Brenda got drunk at the party and passed out. She woke up to the sound of the baby crying. She could hear it, but she could not find it because she was so drunk. Finally, after stumbling around she located the baby. She had trouble getting the baby's bottle organized and had a terrible time trying to feed it, as she slowly sobered up.

Something snapped that night. Brenda was utterly horrified at herself. She had seen herself as worthless, begging for approval and acceptance, but she had not seen herself as irresponsible. She was embarrassed and ashamed of what she now saw so clearly. "It was one thing to ruin my life, but not this baby's life too." That night she made a conscious decision to stop drinking because she knew she was out of control with it.

Brenda not only stopped drinking, but became so repulsed by irresponsibility that responsibility became a prominent quality of what it meant to be an agent of her career, eventually leading to completion of law school and practice as a lawyer. Through the next few years, responsibility was a guiding theme, enabling her to make further resolutions.

At a dinner party one evening, E gave a drunken guest his car keys to drive home. Brenda refused to sleep in the same bed as E that night because she was so shocked and disgusted with his irresponsible behavior. Irresponsibility was one thing she would not tolerate in herself, nor would she tolerate it in anyone else. Brenda had never taken a stand like this before. The next day E was ashamed of himself and looked to Brenda for forgiveness. For the first time, she saw clearly what a lost cause E was, just as she had seen herself more clearly after her irresponsible act. She deserved more than what E had to offer her. It was the beginning of the end of their stormy marriage.

These descriptions depict a range of resolution experiences, from reflective examination to intense emotional reactions. No doubt they overlap with or blend in with other categories such as emergence, at least in some experiences. However, they differ in the sense that individuals are able to detach from some aspect of the negative story such as a reaction, an emotion, or a behavior. Whatever power a remnant had over one's life, it is severely weakened or dissolved altogether.

Scenario of Destruction

By a one-sided emphasis upon the ways that a negative story loses power in a life, our intent has been to establish the importance of a scenario of destruction in transformation accounts. To this end, we have attempted to portray types of scenes in which the dominant narrative function was to weaken the negative plot. The clarity of these scenes, their frequency and prominence as pivotal events, supports their importance in transforming from a patient to an agent.

Becoming an agent of one's course of life cannot be adequately described as just the growth or enhancement of a sense of agency. Rather, it involved a transformation from one orientation toward living to another orientation. In such a transformation, the power of one story or orientation must be destroyed for the other story to develop and reign. One plot must fade while the other forms. However, the old story does not just slip away. As the scenes amply demonstrate, the old story must be actively disengaged. And that requirement establishes the necessity for a scenario of progressive destruction.

6 / A NARRATIVE OF AGENCY

While preceding chapters have been concerned with the pattern of transformation, the present chapter is concerned with the product, what people became. Given the cases presented, what is the nature of an agent? The clearest instances of what people became can be found in completing experiences such as Ray's fishing trip, Tom's decision to marry, and Carol's sermon. These experiences functioned as ends or completions of the transformation and as personal teaching stories that portrayed for each individual what it was to be an agent. Using these stories, the aim of this chapter is to elaborate basic propositions that distinguish and clarify living as an agent rather than a patient.

An Agent Is Oriented toward the Actualization of Ideals

In an agentic plot, the general aim is to actualize a more ideal state of affairs, to move from what is to what ought to be. The beginning involves a gap between what exists and what is ideally possible, drawing from the person's vision of a good life. If successful, the end involves making an ideal possibility actual. For Ray, fishing was part of the good life, a recovery of what was lost. For Tom, marriage was part of an ideal future that he had thought was no longer possible. For Carol, delivering a sermon was a central part of the life she sought in the clergy. Within literature, an agentic story would be classified as romance, using Frye's (1957) topology. Within psy-

167

chology, an agentic story is closely aligned with what Maddi (1980) termed the perfection theories of personality. A successful end to an agentic story is apt to be exalting. One is elevated by the enactment of it.

By contrast, a patient is oriented more toward avoiding negative possibilities. Success is a matter of what did not happen or was prevented from happening. Or if motivated by an ideal, a patient is not committed to making it actual. One might yearn, daydream, wish, and the like. Patients might move toward the actualization of an ideal through lying and cheating, but this is not the same. For example, when Lee lied that he was a college graduate and a professional, he was certainly able to experience some of the benefits, but what stood out as an actualization was still the deceit. It was not authentic and he had to worry about someone finding out. For lack of a better term, the existence of a patient is messy, filled as it is with confusion of shadow and substance, wish and intention. The existence of an agent seems more clean and direct, striving to make more ideal possibilities fully actual in one's everyday living.

Actualization Depends on Action

The essential, distinctive feature of an agentic plot is that success depends upon action. While a multitude of factors might figure in a story (fickle fate, timely encounters, unexpected support, etc.) it is action that brings something about. This emphasis upon action separates an agentic plot from an indefinite number of other plots that offer rival accounts, convictions about how things come about. For example, dreaming, intensity of want, rescue by others, true love, luck, destiny, pure thoughts, popularity, and the like, might be highlighted as the way things happen. While these factors might enter into an agentic plot, they would be subordinate to action. Action, active participation in the affairs of the world, simply dominates as the way to actualize a more ideal existence.

This conviction about the way things work differs somewhat from conceptions such as Seligman's (1991) learned optimism, Bandura's (1989) self-efficacy, or Rotter's (1966) internal locus of control. Each of these conceptions involves a belief that one can influence outcomes. However, a conviction that actualizations depend upon action is both broader and more basic. For example, a person might have little confidence, but still believe that action is the way to make things happen. Tom started his projects not with a strong belief that he could shape events as he wished, but with the conviction that if ever his situation were to change, he must act. Without taking action, nothing would happen.

Consider a relatively simple goal such as getting a good grade in a course. An agent would not deny that several factors might influence the grade, but would be convinced that action is the most trusted and reliable way to bring a good grade about. Thus, an agent might plan, schedule, study, set priorities, make crucial choices, and so on. That the person is also confident of his or her ability to act effectively to earn a good grade is more like a bonus or boost, but it rests upon the more fundamental conviction about the way good things happen.

Actualization Depends on the Quality of Action

While it is generally accurate that agents rely upon action to get things done, more precisely, they rely upon the *quality* of action. Planning in itself does not forward the end, but good planning does. Deciding in itself does not forward success, but a well-deliberated decision does. Means in themselves do not forward a happy outcome, but adequate, reasonable means do. An emphasis upon quality offers refinements of a basic agentic plot, allowing it to be filled out with an indefinite number of principles or guides for a living as an agent.

As one illustration, Tom learned that uncertainty and lack of specificity in goal setting decreased his commitment to practice. In discussion with his father, he came to the stunning realization that he was responsible for setting and pursuing goals. Still later, he learned the importance of an attitude that anything is possible, of dropping a facade in considering goals (in his case, a facade of independence and invulnerability), of taking risks, of honest examination of one's motives, and of concern for the perspective of others. Each addition involved a refinement of agentic plotting in his own life, at least some of which are apt to apply to any agent. An agentic orientation is an expanding sphere of meaning that continues to evolve. Because the quality of actions is indefinitely analyzable, there is no obvious end to the extensions and refinements that might be made.

A principle is like the moral of a story, standing in the same relationship as a proverb does to a fable. According to Schank (1990), "the concept of indexing is strongly related to the formation of a proverb" (p. 104). An index involves cues or labels for a story that will allow a person to retrieve it later. In Schank's view, an index is composed of a theme (what the story is about—the topic), goal, plan, result, and lesson (conclusion about life from the story), all of which can be neatly and pointedly summed up in a proverb. The formation of a proverb (the meaning of a story) not only serves to index a story, but also expresses a conviction about life from an individual's perspective (Arnold 1962). A well-formed proverb reflects a story and reflects or fits within one's larger orientation to living. As encapsulated, a proverb functions to warn, confront, guide, and inspire the person in future enactments (Adler's seminal crystallization 1956).

While a principle reflects a story like a pointed summary of a plot, it can be used as but part of another story or enactment. For example, Tom learned that unspecified goals within a context of uncertainty undermined steady practice. He can recall a series of experiences that demonstrate this conviction. In future enactments, however, setting specific goals figured in stories, but did not (at least ordinarily) constitute those stories. Once drawn out, a principle might function like a whole plot. In this sense, a person develops a connected repertoire of plots. Ordinarily, however, principles become nested or embedded within larger stories, as ground supports figure. Thus, a rich agentic story such as a completion experience encompasses a number of principles, in support of perhaps a novel proverb. Elaboration of an agentic plot involved this kind of progressive enfoldment of principles that are to be unfolded in enactments.

An Agentic Orientation Is Composed of Bipolar Principles

An orientation is bipolar in the sense that some principles warn, teaching a person what to avoid, while some principles guide, teaching a person what to enact. For example, Beth learned early a plot in which independent actions were punished. At first, this conviction was probably an unqualified assertion about life generally. However, as she came to understand different types of people, and to typecast her father, the principle was probably sharpened, as in the following: When under the authority of a tyrant, independent actions are apt to be punished. For years, this principle was a warning. It stated the way things seemed to her, but not as something positive one would want to follow. Quite the contrary, one would avoid independent actions or avoid tyrants. In contrast, positive principles are directly followed. For example, Ray adopted the general principle that reasonable goals can be achieved. Within his context in which little seemed possible, this principle (nearly a tautology really) was liberating, releasing him from unreal and unattainable expectations to devote himself to what could be achieved.

Often, a principle is constructed with reference to an opposing principle. When Tom learned that uncertainty and unspecific goals led to haphazard efforts and little improvement, it immediately invoked the opposite principle: Sustained effort and improvement follow from goals that are specific, challenging, and possible. He adopted the latter while avoiding the former. However, other principles do not necessarily have a direct opposite. For example, what is the opposite to Beth's principle that tyrants punish independent action? Many contrasts seem possible. For example, when under the authority of a benevolent person, independent actions are rewarded, or when outside the influence of a tyrant, independent actions are unrestrained. That an oppositional tendency is operative seems evident, but this does not mean that an opposing principle can be easily or definitely identified. Indeed, it might take years for a person to work out what opposing principle is valid or it might even be left indefinitely in suspense.

One pole of the repertoire of principles stems from the old story while the other pole stems from the new story in formation. While persons might draw from movies, novels, anecdotes, and a wide array of cultural material, principles are most forcefully anchored in the life history of the person. Inevitably, such an orientation evolves in distinctive ways. For example, Brenda's enactment of agency emphasized moral responsibility. Accompanying her growing sense of responsibility were such emotions as revulsion, indignation, and anger. There was a somewhat different basis for her rise in agency that gives her repertoire a distinctive tone.

Comparing the sense of agency of two persons is not like comparing height, but more like comparing two novels. The principles (proverbs, morals of stories) evident in two orientations differ in scope, vulnerability, specificity, range, balance, cohesion, and adaptability, among other things. Nevertheless, Arnold (1962) has clearly demonstrated how quantitative comparisons can be made. Using her manual, the principles of living that are identified as representative of an orientation can be scored and summed to provide an overall score. Her manual for categorizing and scoring principles can certainly be improved, particularly in light of agency theorists such as Maddi (1988), Seligman (1991), and Bandura (1989), but it provides an ingenious and fruitful beginning that has already received strong validation in correlational studies.

An Agentic Enactment Represents a Way of Life

The basic plot of agency is rather straightforward. To attain a valued end, a person takes action and overcomes various forms of resistance. However, this basic plot does not seem to be enough to count as a manifestation of agency. An essential part of what makes a plot agentic is its relation to a larger story in which it is embedded, like a chapter in a novel. An action has significance, if it both forwards and constitutes in miniature the larger story of one's life as an agent actualizing a unique life plot.

Given completion experiences from the case studies, that which is to be actualized in an enactment is fraught with meaning for a way of life. For Ray, being able to go fishing (or more generally, to participate in outdoor recreation) was part of the good life, part of what made life precious in growing up, a recovery of what he had lost, and a symbol of his independence. To go fishing not only forwarded the kind of person he wanted to be and the kind of life he wanted to live, but constituted that person and life in immediate circumstances. For Tom, marriage was part of the ideal future he had thought was out of reach. For Carol, delivering a sermon was a central enactment of her ideal vocation. Each enactment was an immediate, partial actualization of the good life, and an experience filled with promise.

The obstacles each person faced and overcame also figured significantly as general (or symbolic) barriers in the person's life. The obstacles were or symbolized barriers that stood between the person and the good life. For example, Ray was faced with physical dependence, Tom with interdependence that could penetrate his mask of invulnerability, and Carol with the threat of exposure and embarrassment. Overcoming such barriers was meaningful in itself and meaningful as a more general or symbolic victory over those kinds of barriers threatening to confine one's future.

The way each person achieved a goal and overcame resistance was the style of action expected or required in one's future plan of living. Ray's experience stressed physical exertion, resourcefulness, and individuality. Tom stressed honest deliberation, breadth of perspective, and commitment despite fear. Carol stressed expression, authenticity, and belonging. The personal qualities emphasized tended to be precisely those that boded well for the kind of life being shaped. Ray's future life required demanding physical effort and challenge. Tom's life demanded thoughtful and broad deliberation, planning and deciding. Carol's future required communication and empathic understanding. The qualities needed for a way of life seem to be strongly validated in immediate action.

In summary, an enactment is agentic when it reflects a desired way of life. Some enactments are virtual prototypes or paradigm cases of what it is to live a certain way. Some enactments are borderline cases and some are irrelevant. A paradigm case radiates with significance; an irrelevant case does not. For example, if Carol went on a fishing trip alone, it would not mean what it did to Ray. Indeed, it would probably be irrelevant, lacking as it does in what makes up agency in her way of life. Even though an enactment appeared to involve powerful actions, overcoming resistance and success, it would not necessarily constitute a very strong demonstration or experience of agency, and might not count much at all. Significance varies with the extent to which enactments are paradigmatic of a way of life, and this significance seems to be part of what is necessary to experience a sense of agency. It is this significance that makes a sense of agency personal, fraught with meaning in an individual life history.

Performing the Role of an Agent Is to Enact an Agentic Plot

The roles of an agent and a patient in a story are quite different. An agent makes a plot move along by what he or she does. To a significant extent, the plot is enacted. In contrast, a patient suffers, undergoes, or allows a plot to unfold. No active effort in shaping events is required or effective. After his accident, Tom felt like a "total leech," envisioning a life in which he would continually receive, but never give or contribute. While he dreaded this prospect, there seemed to be nothing he could do to avoid it. The role of a leech had been forced upon him. To perform the role of a patient is to experience a plot unfolding that one can do little to avert. Indeed, Tom's self-deprecation and feelings of worthlessness began to suit him for his role. However, to perform the role of an agent is to enact the plot or at least contribute significantly to the course it takes. Without the active effort of the person, the plot does not go on. Certainly, a person might be active in taking the role of a victim or patient, but it is not necessary. However, to be an agent, active effort is necessary.

The qualities of an agent are those that are required for the role to be performed and the plot to be enacted. Different kinds of agentic plots call for different kinds of knowledge, virtue, and skill. Ray's course of life required physical strength while Tom and Carol's did not. Carol's course of life required biblical knowledge while Ray's did not. While there are common qualities for agents generally, other qualities are salient only in a particular course of life. Tritely put, to be an agent in a physics laboratory, one would have to know a lot about physics, yet such knowledge is not generally necessary to be an agent. Whatever the qualities uniquely suited to a way of life, they are what enable a person to fulfill an agentic role in a course of life.

In one sense, a person must be reasonably successful to be an agent. If one were unable to actualize a course of action successfully, one would not be fulfilling an agentic role, nor living an agentic plot. Rather, one would be living a failed enactment or some other plot. Successful actualization of an agentic role and plot is not the same as a successful end. For example, if Tom only breathed on his own for twenty-eight seconds when his goal was thirty seconds, he might have regarded the outcome as unsuccessful. But still, he might have enacted the role of an agent in practice. He made happen what would not have happened without his effort. Nevertheless, the end is often used to gauge the whole enactment, and can wrongly undermine a sense of agency. While the end is certainly important, the distinction here is quite basic and crucial. Primarily, a person is agentic if he or she can successfully actualize an agentic role and plot. Then, the person can truly be said to be living as an agent rather than a patient. Only secondarily does a successful end figure into agency, increasing confidence.

If a person viewed his or her performance of an agentic role sheerly as means to an end, the outcome would be decisive. Means are of value in forwarding an end, but are not necessarily of value in themselves (Aristotle 1980). Thus, if the outcome were unsuccessful, the whole experience would lack meaning. However, no one in the case studies regarded an agentic role sheerly as means, as only of value if one were successful. While a successful outcome was certainly yearned for, performance of an agentic role was an end in itself, a good in itself. It was an intrinsically motivated activity (e.g., Csikszentmihalyi 1990; Deci 1975). So pronounced is this feature in enactments that we would not regard a person as an agent, or at least not a full agent, if performance of the role were merely an extrinsically motivated activity.

Consider Ray as one example. He was utterly repulsed by the model of a broken man who deadened himself to the world. Ray enacted his role as a polar opposite. Even if he did not succeed often, it felt better to have strived than to have done nothing. As an agent, he felt more control, more optimistic, more involved, just more alive. Acting as an agent was a partial and immediate actualization of the kind of person he wanted to be. As he developed, agency became elaborated as a strand of identity, incorporating fundamental evaluations of self and world. That is, at some point in his transformation, he could not act as a patient and remain himself. Agency and identity were bound together and became difficult to distinguish. The role of an agent becomes an agentic identity. For this reason, these persons seem more resilient to setbacks, criticisms, flaws, and failures. If instead, agentic performance were extrinsically motivated, sheerly a means that is dependent on outcome for value, no such stability would be expected.

An Agentic Enactment Is Supported by Context

Throughout the accounts, it is striking how busy individuals were in leaving, entering, shaping, and adjusting to settings, relationships, roles, and activities. This impressive investment of time, energy, attention, and resources was well-placed, for if the context were not suitable, then a person could not act as an agent or act fully as an agent. From comparing experiences at the beginning and end of accounts, a major difference is that an agent is allowed, supported, or encouraged to act as an agent while a patient is influenced to act as a patient, or at least hindered from being more active. An enactment of agency is so thoroughly contextualized that context can be said to co-constitute the performance.

Consider Carol's sermon. She was supplied with a setting that was uniquely suited for delivering sermons. She did not have to stand on a box in a park or plaza, or struggle with the myriad of difficulties that emerge in trying to do something outside of a proper setting (e.g., imagine trying to deliver a sermon in a movie theater when people are watching the movie). Her relations were supportive. Friends encouraged her and offered guidance. The priest was positive. The audience was receptive. The role she took was a well-defined one and others played their parts in complementary roles. The activity was clearly defined, governed by a public script in which she and others could participate. Given her life-historical context, the activity of preaching in a church was extremely meaningful, connected to other meaningful possibilities in religious work. And the things that dotted the setting all supported her performance. She had the proper attire. Music led up to her sermon. There were pews, Bibles, and so on. So strong is the force of context that it is difficult to conceive of Carol delivering a sermon outside of an appropriate one, and that is why context co-constitutes performance.

This claim does not contradict claims that stress the power of individuals. For example, one might reasonably claim that a person's character is really shown in adverse or unfavorable circumstances, or that agency is really shown in novel settings in which a person must shape a role and way of acting. Far from disclaiming the importance of context, as is sometimes tacitly indicated, both implicitly support the potency of context. People do not perform in a vacuum. There are real settings, relationships, things, activities, and the like that help encage and disempower or liberate and empower. Agency is not just a matter of confidence or optimism or any personal attribute, but of contextual strands that shape a person's course of life and enable agentic enactments.

Consider, for instance, a novelist whose novels have been rejected by publishers for several years. The situation is adverse, but this does not mean the context is either irrelevant or overcome. Quite the contrary, in cases we have studied, context remains critical. For example, there might not be anything actually preventing a person from writing. The person has pen, ink, paper, and can find the time to do it. There might be others who encourage, support, or at least allow one's efforts. The person might have a degree in English literature or models of a struggling artist to follow. His or her working area might be surrounded by novels, supportive material, and symbols. In short, writing a novel under adverse circumstances is as thoroughly contextualized as Carol's sermon.

Agency and Narrative

Perhaps there are tasks such as throwing darts or solving an algorithm in which the meaning of agency can be reduced to confidence or some other attribute. But tasks such as these, usually so outside of the course of life, are strangely anomalous experiences, at least for most people. For the life of a person, they are apt to be devoid of meaningful implications. In contrast, the topic of this study has been tasks or activities that are fraught with meaningful implications such that a person feels like the agent of his or her course of life. This is a different order of investigation, one that requires an understanding of a person in characteristic contexts that inform a course of life. Necessarily, the topic has expanded, always threatening to become unwieldy, and we are searching here for an apt clarification of what an agent is, given the scope and depth of ideas the accounts seemed to require.

An agentic performance involves a dramatization of oneself and the world. The immediate setting becomes a scene in which a person must maintain a definition of oneself and the situation. From a riverbank to a hospital rule, elements of the scene assume importance to the extent that they impede the agents progress or help it along. Other people are cast in roles and aligned on one side or the other, protagonistic or antagonistic. The immediate drama or story is embedded in and reflects a larger story of one's course of life (e.g., as teaching a class might reflect the life of a teacher). In short, a person must actualize in definite settings a whole configuration of meaning. That configuration of meaning involves a role, a plot that pivots on action, and context.

To be an agent is to be emplotted in an agentic narrative that is lived. That is, to describe what individuals were like at the end of the transformation, the most striking summary is that they went about living agentic stories, full experiences with a beginning, middle, and end. This descriptive statement is composed of two parts. First, individuals follow an agentic plot. As an instance of what Harre (1974) termed a powerful particular, a real structure that exists at a time and is unfolded in a patterned way over time, a plot is a formal cause. It accounts for the form that is manifested. Second, in following an agentic plot, individuals encounter novel difficulties, ambiguous roles, realities that do not quite fit, and differences in actualizing a plot. Due to novelties and differences, actualizing a plot is patterned but never quite the same from one instance to the next. The emphasis upon a "narrative that is lived" requires or presumes further evolution and development of an agentic orientation. To capture this more dynamic aspect of agency, one might say a person has reached authorship. *An agent is a person who has become the author of his or her course of life as an ongoing composition.*

Bibliography

Adler, Alfred (1956). *The individual psychology of Alfred Adler.* Edited by H. Ansbacher and R. Ansbacher. New York: Basic Books.

Allport, Gordon (1955). *Becoming: Basic considerations for a psychology of personality.* New Haven, Conn.: Yale University Press.

Allport, Gordon (1961). *Pattern and growth in personality.* New York: Holt, Rinehart and Winston.

Andrisani, P. J., and Nestel, G. (1976). Internal-external control as a contributor and outcome of work experience. *Journal of Applied Psychology* 76: 156–65.

Arendt, Hannah (1978). *The life of the mind: Thinking.* New York: Harcourt, Brace, Jovanovich.

Aristotle (1980). *The nichomachean ethics.* Translated by D. Ross. Oxford: Oxford University Press.

Arnheim, Rudolf (1986). The two faces of gestalt psychology. *American Psychologist* 41: 820–24.

Arnold, Magda (1962). *Story sequence analysis.* New York: Columbia University Press.

Avasthi, Surabhi (1990). Helping people cope with the trauma of layoffs. *Guidepost* 33: no. 7: 1.

Bandura, Albert (1977). Self-efficacy: Toward a unifying theory of behavioral change. *Psychological Review* 84: 191–215.

Bandura, Albert (1989). Human agency in social cognitive theory. *American Psychologist* 44: 1175–84.

Bandura, Alberta (1989). Self-regulation of motivation and action through internal standards and goal systems. In *Goal concepts in personality and social psychology,* edited by L. Perrin, pp. 19–86. Hillsdale, N.J.: Lawrence Erlbaum.

Britton, James (1970). *Language and learning*. Baltimore: Penquin Books.

Bruner, Jerome (1987). Life as narrative. *Social Research* 54: 11–32.

Burke, Kenneth (1969). *A grammar of motives*. Berkeley: University of California Press.

Carr, David (1986). *Time, narrative and history*. Indianapolis: Indiana University Press.

Casanova, Giovanni (1984). *The life and memoirs of Casanova*. Ttranslated by A. Machen, edited by G. Gribble. New York: Da Capo.

Charme, S. L. (1984). *Meaning and myth in the study of lives*. Philadelphia: University of Pennsylvania Press.

Chusid, Hanna, and Cochran, Larry (1989). The meaning of career change from the perspective of family roles and dramas. *Journal of Counseling Psychology* 36: 34–41.

Cochran, Larry (1985). *Position and nature of personhood*. Westport, Conn.: Greenwood Press.

Cochran, Larry (1986). *Portrait and Story*. Westport, Conn.: Greenwood Press.

Cochran, Larry (1990). *The sense of vocation: A study of life and career development*. Albany, N.Y.: State University of New York Press.

Csikszentmihalyi, Mihaly (1975). *Beyond boredom and anxiety*. San Francisco: Jossey-Bass.

Csikszentmihalyi, Mihaly (1990). *Flow: The psychology of optimal experience*. New York: Harper and Row.

Csikszentmihalyi, Mihaly, and Beattie, Olga (1979). Life themes: A theoretical and empirical exploration of their origins and effects. *Journal of Humanistic Psychology* 19: 45–63.

Csikszentmihalyi, Mihaly, and Csikszentmihalyi, Isabella (1988). *Optimal experience: Psychological studies of flow in consciousness*. New York: Cambridge University Press.

Danto, Arthur (1985). *Narration and knowledge*. New York: Columbia University Press.

deCharms, Richard (1968). *Personal causation*. New York: Academic Press.

deCharms, Richard (1976). *Enhancing motivation in the classroom*. New York: Irvington.

deCharms, Richard (1981). Personal causation and locus of control: Two different traditions and two uncorrelated measures. In *Research with the locus of control construct (Vol. 1): Assessment methods*, edited by H. Lefcourt, pp. 337–58. New York: Academic Press.

de Charms, Richard (1984). Motivation enhancement in educational settings. In *Research on motivation in education (Vol. 1): Student motivation*, edited by R. Ames and C. Ames, pp. 275–310. New York: Academic Press.

de Charms, Richard (1987a). The burden of motivation. In *Advances in motivation and achievement: Enhancing motivation*, edited by M. Maehr and D. Kleiber, pp. 1–21. London: JAI Press.

de Charms, Richard (1987b). Personal causation, agency, and the self. In *The book of the self: Person, pretext and process*, edited by P. Young-Eisendrath and J. Hall, pp. 17–41. New York: University Press.

Deci, Edward (1975). *Intrinsic motivation*. New York: Plenum.

Eliade, Mircea (1958). *Rites and symbols of initiation*. New York: Harper and Row.

Ellis, W. D. (1967). *A source book of gestalt psychology*. New York: Humanities Press.

Erikson, Erik (1959). *Identity and the life cycle*. New York: International Universities Press.

Foucault, Michel (1980). *Power/knowledge: Selected interviews and other writings*. New York: Pantheon Books.

Frankfurt, H. (1971). Freedom of the will and the concept of a person. *Journal of Philosophy* 67: 5–20.

Freire, Paulo (1982). *Pedagogy of the oppressed*. Translated by M. Ramos. New York: Continuum Publishing.

Frye, Bruce (1967). A letter from Max Weber. *The Journal of Modern History* 39: 119–25.

Frye, Northrup (1957). *The anatomy of criticism*. Princeton: Princeton University Press.

Fuller, Andrew (1990). *Insight into value*. Albany, N.Y.: State University of New York Press.

Garfinkel, Harold (1956). Conditions of successful degradation ceremonies. *The American Journal of Sociology* 61: 420–24.

Ghiselin, Brewster (1955). *The creative process*. New York: Mentor.

Harding, D. W. (1937). The role of the onlooker. *Scrutiny* 6: 247–58.

Harre, Rom (1974). Blueprint for a new science. In *Reconstructing social psychology*, edited by N. Armistead. Baltimore: Penquin Books.

Heath, Douglas (1980). Wanted: A comprehensive model of health development. *The Personnel and Guidance Journal* 59: 391–99.

Howard, George (1989). *A tale of two stories: Excursions into a narrative approach to psychology*. Notre Dame: Academic Publications.

Kelly, George (1955). *The psychology of personal constructs*. New York: Norton.

Kobasa, Suzanne (1979). Stressful life events, personality and health: An inquiry into hardiness. *Journal of Personality and Social Psychology* 37: 1–11.

Kohn, Melvin, and Schooler, Carmi (1983). *Work and personality*. Norwood, N.J.: Ablex.

Lee, Thomas; Locke, Edwin; and Latham, Gary (1989). Goal setting theory and job performance. In *Goal concepts in personality and social psychology*, edited by L. Pervin, pp. 291–326. Hillsdale, N.J.: Lawrence Erlbaum.

Locke, Edwin, and Latham, Gary (1984). *Goal setting: A motivational technique that works*. Englewood Cliffs, N.J.: Prentice-Hall.

McAdams, Dan (1985). *Power, intimacy and the life story*. Homewood, Ill.: Dorsey Press.

McCall, George, and Simmons, J. L. (1978). *Indentities and interactions*. New York: Free Press.

McClelland, David (1961). *The achieving society*. Princetion, N.J.: Van Nostrand.

McClelland, David (1965). Toward a theory of motive acquisition. *American Psychologist* 20: 321–33.

MacGregor, Anne, and Cochran, Larry (1988). Work as enactment of family drama. *Career Development Quarterly* 37: 138–48.

MacIntyre, Alasdair (1984). *After virtue*. Notre Dame: University of Notre Dame Press.

Maddi, Salvatore (1970). The search for meaning. In *Nebraska symposium on motivation*, edited by M. Page. Lincoln, Nebr. University of Nebraska Press.

Maddi, Salvatore (1980). *Personality theories: A comparative analysis*. 4th ed. Homewood, Ill.: Dorsey Press.

Maddi, Salvatore (1988). On the problem of accepting facticity and pursuing possibility. In *Hermeneutics and psychological theory: Interpretive perspectives on personality, psychotherapy and psychopathology*, edited by S. Messer; L. Sass; and R. Woolfolk, pp. 182–209. New Brunswick, N.J.: Rutgers University Press.

Manicas, Peter, and Secord, Paul (1983). Implications for psychology of a new philosophy of science. *American Psychologist* 38: 399–413.

Mill, John (1969). *Autobiography and other writings*, edited by J. Stillinger. Boston: Houghton Mifflin.

Murray, Henry (1943). *Thematic Appreception Test*. Cambridge: Harvard University Press.

Neimeyer, Robert (1987). An orientation to personal construct therapy. In *Personal construct therapy casebook*, edited by R. Neimeyer and G. Neimeyer, pp. 3–19. New York: Springer Publishing.

Ochberg, Richard (1987). *Middle aged sons and the meaning of work*. Ann Arbor, Mich: UMI Research Press.

Osherson, Samuel (1980). *Holding on and letting go*. New York: Free Press.

Peale, Norman (1984). *The true joy of positive living: An autobiography*. New York: Morrow.

Peele, Stanton (1983). *The science of experience*. Lexington, Mass.: D. C. Heath

Piaget, Jean (1968). *Six psychological studies*. New York: Vintage.

Polanyi, Michael (1967). *The tacit dimension*. Garden City, N.Y.: Anchor Books.

Polkinghorne, Donald (1988). *Narrative knowing and the human sciences*. Albany, N.Y.: State University of New York Press.

Ricoeur, Paul (1984). *Time and narrative*. Translated by K. McLaughlin and D. Pellauer. Chicago: University of Chicago Press.

Rotter, Julian (1966). Generalized expectancies for internal versus external control of reinforcement. *Journal of Consulting and Clinical Psychology* 43: 56–67.

Rotter, Julian (1975). Some problems and misconceptions related to the construct of internal versus external control of reinforcement. *Journal of Consulting and Clinical Psychology* 43: 56–67.

Saint Augustine (1961). *Confessions*. Translated by R. S. Pine-Coffin. Baltimore: Penguin Books.

Sarbin, Theodore (1986). *Narrative psychology*. New York: Praeger.

Sartre, Jean Paul (1966). *Being and nothingness*. Translated by Hazel Barnes. New York: Pocket Books.

Schank, Roger (1990). *Tell me a story*. New York: Charles Scribner's Sons.

Seligman, Martin (1975). *Helplessness*. San Francisco: W. H. Freeman.

Seligman, Martin (1991). *Learned optimism*. New York: Alfred A. Knopf.

Sloan, Tod (1986). *Deciding: Self-deception in life choices*. New York: Metheun.

Spence, Donald (1982). *Narrative truth and historical truth: Meaning and interpretation in psychoanalysis*. New York: Norton.

Spivack, George; Platt, Jerome; and Shure, Myrna (1976). *The problem-solving approach to adjustment*. San Francisco: Jossey-Bass.

Steffens, Lincoln (1931). *The autobiography of Lincoln Steffens*. New York: Harcourt, Brace and Company.

Stephenson, William (1953). *The study of behavior*. Chicago: University of Chicago Press.

Taylor, Charles (1977). What is human agency? In *The Self: Psychological and philosophical issues*, edited by T. Mischel, pp. 103–35. Totowa, N.J.: Rowman and Littlefield.

Turner, Victor (1974). *Dramas, fields and metaphors*. Ithaca: Cornell University Press.

Turner, Victor, and Bruner, Edward (1986). *The anthropology of experience*. Chicago: University of Illinois Press.

Van Gennep, Arnold (1960). *The rites of passage*. Chicago: University of Chicago Press.

Washington, Booker (1956). *Up from slavery*. New York: Bantam.

Werkmeister, W. (1967). *Man and his values*. Lincoln: University of Nebraska Press.

Weston, Harold (1970). *Form in literature: A theory of technique and construction*. Edinburgh: Edinburgh Press.

White, Michael, and Epston, David (1990). *Narrative means to therapeutic ends*. New York: Norton.

White, Robert (1959). Motivation reconsidered: The concept of competence. *Psychological Review* 66: 297–333.

Willis, Paul (1977). *Learning to Labor*. New York: Columbia University Press.

Wright, Beatrice (1983). *Physical disability—A psychosocial approach*. New York: Harper and Row.

Yin, Robert (1984). *Case study research: Design and methods*. Beverly Hills: Sage Publications.

Index